Issues in the
Environment

Other books in the Contemporary Issues series:

Biomedical Ethics
Sports

CONTEMPORARY ISSUES

Issues in the
Environment

by Patricia D. Netzley

Lucent Books, San Diego, CA

With thanks to my parents, Marge and George Faber, for their faith and encouragement; to my husband, Raymond, for his love and support; and to my children, Matthew, Sarah, and Jacob, for their patience and cooperation.

Library of Congress Cataloging-in-Publication Date

Netzley, Patricia D.
  The environment / by Patricia D. Netzley.
    p. cm.—(Contemporary issues series)
  Includes bibliographical references and index.
  ISBN 1-56006-475-7 (alk. paper)
    1. Environmentalism—United States. 2. Environmental protection—
Economic aspects—United States. 3. Environmental law—United
States. I. Title. II. Series: Contemporary issues series (San Diego,
Calif.)
GE197.N48 1998
333.7—dc21   97-25894
                                                                  CIP

TABLE OF CONTENTS

Foreword

When men are brought face to face with their opponents, forced to listen and learn and mend their ideas, they cease to be children and savages and begin to live like civilized men. Then only is freedom a reality, when men may voice their opinions because they must examine their opinions.

Walter Lippmann, American editor and writer

CONTROVERSY FOSTERS DEBATE. The very mention of a controversial issue prompts listeners to choose sides and offer opinion. But seeing beyond one's opinions is often difficult. As Walter Lippmann implies, true reasoning comes from the ability to appreciate and understand a multiplicity of viewpoints. This ability to assess the range of opinions is not innate; it is learned by the careful study of an issue. Those who wish to reason well, as Lippmann attests, must be willing to examine their own opinions even as they weigh the positive and negative qualities of the opinions of others.

The *Contemporary Issues* series explores controversial topics through the lens of opinion. The series addresses some of today's most debated issues and, drawing on the diversity of opinions, presents a narrative that reflects the controversy surrounding those issues. All of the quoted testimonies are taken from primary sources and represent both prominent and lesser-known persons who have argued these topics. For example, the title on biomedical ethics contains the views of physicians commenting on both sides of the physician-assisted suicide issue: Some wage a moral argument that assisted suicide allows patients to die with dignity, while others assert that assisted suicide violates the Hippocratic oath. Yet the book also includes the opinions of those who see the issue in a more personal way. The relative of a person who died by assisted suicide feels the loss of a loved one and makes a plaintive cry against it, while companions of another assisted suicide victim attest that their friend no longer wanted to endure the agony of a slow death. The profusion of quotes illustrates the range of thoughts and emotions that impinge on any debate. Displaying the range of perspectives, the series is designed to show how personal belief—whether informed by statistical evidence, religious conviction, or public opinion—shapes and complicates arguments.

Each title in the *Contemporary Issues* series discusses multiple controversies within a single field of debate. The title on environmental issues, for example, contains one chapter that asks whether the Endangered Species Act should be repealed, while another asks if Americans can afford the economic and social costs of environmentalism. Narrowing the focus of debate to a specific question, each chapter sharpens the competing perspectives and investigates the philosophies and personal convictions that inform these viewpoints.

Students researching contemporary issues will find this format particularly useful in uncovering the central controversies of topics by placing them in a moral, economic, or political context that allows the students to easily see the points of disagreement. Because of this structure, the series provides an excellent launching point for further research. By clearly defining major points of contention, the series also aids readers in critically examining the structure and source of debates. While providing a resource on which to model persuasive essays, the quoted opinions also permit students to investigate the credibility and usefulness of the evidence presented.

For students contending with current issues, the ability to assess the credibility, usefulness, and persuasiveness of the testimony as well as the factual evidence given by the quoted experts is critical not only in judging the merits of these arguments but in analyzing the students' own beliefs. By plumbing the logic of another person's opinions, readers will be better able to assess their own thinking. And this, in turn, can promote the type of introspection that leads to a conviction based on reason. Though *Contemporary Issues* offers the opportunity to shape one's own opinions in light of competing or concordant philosophies, above all, it shows readers that well-reasoned, well-intentioned arguments can be countered by opposing opinions of equal worth.

Critically examining one's own opinions as well as the opinions of others is what Walter Lippmann believes makes an individual "civilized." Developing the skill early can only aid a reader's understanding of both moral conviction and political action. For students, a facility for reasoning is indispensable. Comprehending the foundations of opinions leads the student to the heart of controversy—to a recognition of what is at stake when holding a certain viewpoint. But the goal is not detached analysis; the issues are often far too immediate for that. The *Contemporary Issues* series induces the reader not only to see the shape of a current controversy, but to engage it, to respond to it, and ultimately to find one's place within it.

Introduction

Environmental Protections and the U.S. Economy

I N 1996, PRICE PFISTER, A MANUFACTURER of household faucets, decided to relocate its southern California operation to Mexico. The company then laid off three hundred American employees and scheduled the termination of another three hundred for the following year.

Price Pfister saved money by relocating, because labor in Mexico is far cheaper than in the United States. Stacy Finz, in a February 1, 1997, article for the *Los Angeles Daily News*, quotes former Price Pfister worker Roberto Navarret's wage comparison: "At Price Pfister [in California], I made $9.11 an hour. In Mexico that's what I'd make for the whole day." But after twenty-six years in California, what made the company suddenly decide to take such a drastic step to save money?

According to Barry Stavro's September 24, 1996, *Los Angeles Times* article, "Price Pfister Makes Cuts to Meet State Rules," the high cost of environmentalism forced relocation. In January 1996 the company settled an environmental lawsuit by agreeing to pay $2.4 million in civil penalties, attorney's fees, and environmental education and research. To defray the expense of judgment and legal fees, the company replaced American workers with Mexican ones.

Regulating a Hazardous Substance

One plaintiff in the lawsuit was the state of California, which accused Price Pfister of not complying with state regulations regarding the use of lead in faucets. At one time faucets manufactured in California were allowed to contain specified amounts of this metal.

Then the state mandated its removal not only from faucets but from many other household products as well.

In compound form, lead appears in paints as white or yellow pigment, and it is a component of certain types of crystal glassware. Because it resists corrosive attack by air, water, and several chemicals, it is also applied to iron and steel pipes and faucets to protect them from rust.

But lead is poisonous to human beings, who can ingest the element in food, water, or airborne particles. The body can only expel lead through the slow process of hair and fingernail growth. In the meantime, the element accumulates in blood, tissue, and bone. High levels of lead in the body are known to cause kidney damage, nerve damage, strokes, convulsions, paralysis, brain damage, and even death. Therefore, California has restricted how much lead its communities can allow in their drinking water, and in 1986 the state's voters passed Proposition 65, an initiative that set the acceptable level of lead, as well as other hazardous substances, in any manufactured product as one-thousandth of the lowest dose that proved

Engineers from the Environmental Protection Agency test for toxins at Love Canal in Niagara Falls. Government regulations aimed at protecting people are controversial because they are costly and inconvenient.

harmful to animals in laboratory tests.

This limit is controversial. Because lead is toxic to humans only when the body contains a large amount of the metal (and that amount is typically accumulated over a long period of time), scientists disagree about what constitutes a dangerous level of lead from any one source. According to Frank Clifford, "The California standard for lead and other chemicals linked to birth defects has always been controversial. . . . [T]he ill effects of lead result from cumulative intake, often from a variety of sources over a number of years."

Economic Consequences

But whether or not Proposition 65 sets a reasonable limit for lead exposure, the initiative allows the state to sue companies that fail to comply with its standards. Barry Stavro says that the initiative has therefore "led to suits against companies selling everything from fine china to well pumps." The Price Pfister case began in 1992, when the state of California joined two environmental groups, the Natural Resources Defense Council (NRDC) and the Environmental Law Foundation, in a lawsuit against faucet companies whose products were leaching lead into tap water at thirty to forty times the rate allowed by law.

Environmentalists believe that initiatives like Proposition 65 and the lawsuits that result from them are necessary to protect people's health. According to Al Meyerhoff, a senior attorney with the NRDC, the Price Pfister settlement that resulted from his group's lawsuit means "we've hit a home run for public health. . . . [Lead is] one of the most hazardous chemicals known."

But some people believe that economic health also has a direct effect on physical health. In the case of Price Pfister, they point out that former employees are suffering because of the company's relocation. For example, Stacy Finz quotes Mercedes Hernandez, faced with supporting four children: "I can't sleep. The bills are piling up."

Economists Robert Krol and Shirley Svorny argue that the Price Pfister case "illustrates that state regulation has real economic and human costs." Krol and Svorny believe that while "blame has been put on [Price Pfister] management for caring more about profits than their workers [in their decision to move their factory] . . . the blame really belongs on the shoulders of the people of the state of California [for passing Proposition 65]."

These economists argue that companies have an obligation to remain economically healthy: "Most managers would prefer not to fire people. But the reality is that their responsibility is to the long-term survival of the firm."

Experts agree that environmental regulations cost businesses and taxpayers money. Yet they do not agree on whether these regulations actually benefit the environment. Whether the most expensive environmental policies and practices, particularly those involving endangered species, wilderness areas, and trash disposal, are worthwhile remains controversial. Evaluating the costs and benefits surrounding these issues highlights the conflict between economics and environmental reform.

Chapter ▮1▮

Should the Endangered Species Act Be Repealed?

I N THE SOUTHERN UNITED STATES, a small bird is at the center of a large controversy. Called the red-cockaded woodpecker, it nests within self-made cavities of longleaf or loblolly pine trees that are more than eighty years old. It cannot peck its way inside younger, stronger trees.

By some estimates, old-growth longleaf and loblolly pine forests once covered 90 million acres in the eastern and southern United States. Today there are only a few hundred thousand acres left. Consequently, the number of red-cockaded woodpeckers has declined from 1.6 million family groups to 4,500 groups, or 12,000 individual birds. This means that it is a species in danger of extinction and therefore falls under the protection of the Endangered Species Act (ESA).

The ESA was enacted in 1973 by a unanimous vote of the U.S. Congress. It requires that endangered species be identified on a regular basis and that their names be placed on a list. Once a species is placed on the endangered species list, neither it nor its habitat can be harmed. Therefore no one who finds a red-cockaded woodpecker on his or her property can interfere with the bird in any way.

So when Benjamin Cone Jr. of North Carolina wanted to harvest timber from his family's land in 1991, he was dismayed to find that his pine trees housed twenty-nine red-cockaded woodpeckers. Under the Endangered Species Act, this discovery meant that Cone could not touch over eleven hundred of his seventy-two hundred acres. The restricted acreage fell under the control of the U.S. Fish and Wildlife Service, which mandated that a half-mile radius of forest remain undisturbed around every tree inhabited by a woodpecker.

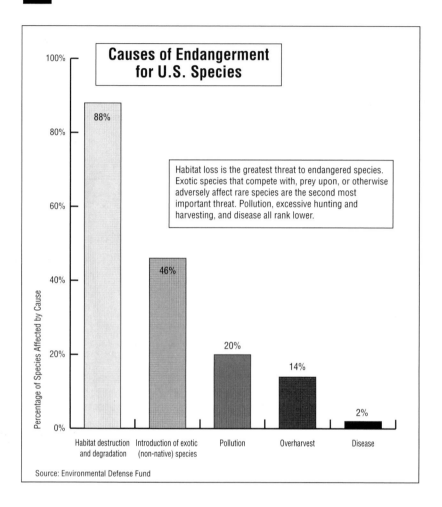

Causes of Endangerment for U.S. Species

Habitat loss is the greatest threat to endangered species. Exotic species that compete with, prey upon, or otherwise adversely affect rare species are the second most important threat. Pollution, excessive hunting and harvesting, and disease all rank lower.

Percentage of Species Affected by Cause

- Habitat destruction and degradation — 88%
- Introduction of exotic (non-native) species — 46%
- Pollution — 20%
- Overharvest — 14%
- Disease — 2%

Source: Environmental Defense Fund

By 1995 Cone had lost the use of more than two thousand of his acres. He has estimated that the red-cockaded woodpecker has cost him over $2 million in lost revenue. But he still has to pay property taxes on the full value of the land as though every acre can be harvested. The government bases the amount of a person's property taxes on how much the piece of land is worth, and it has refused to decrease Cone's taxes to reflect his lost acreage.

Economic Consequences

Situations like Cone's are not unusual. Many other people have suffered economic losses because of the ESA. For instance, in Idaho a federal judge stopped logging, mining, ranching, and road construction on 14 million acres of land because those operations were disturbing three endangered species of salmon that spawn in the rivers there. In San Bernardino County, California, a planned hospital had to be moved 250 feet—at a cost of $3.5 million—when the Delhi Sands fly was listed as endangered. The fly's existence depends on a particular type of flower found to grow on the development site.

In cases like these, not only landowners but farmers, construction workers, and other people who make their livings from the land are hurt when a piece of property becomes a protected habitat. Thomas Lambert, in his article "Endangered Species Act: Facing Swift Opposition" in the March 1996 issue of *USA Today Magazine*, explains:

> The listing of an endangered species can bring an abrupt end to economic activities or require substantial changes to planned development projects. The listing of the northern spotted owl, for instance, has brought an end to logging ventures in many forest areas—both public and private— leading to tens of thousands of job losses and is expected to impose recovery costs [the expense of bringing a species back from extinction] of more than $20,000,000,000.

Such costs lead many people to criticize the ESA as being harmful to the economy. However, Professor Stephen Meyer, director of the Massachusetts Institute of Technology (MIT) Project on Environmental Politics and Policy, argues that the economy is not harmed by species protection. Meyer studied economic growth trends in the United States between 1975 and 1990, specifically examining how the Endangered Species Act affected state economies. His research indicated that states with the largest number of endangered species fared no worse economically than states with few endangered species.

In his article in the August 1995 issue of *Technology Review*, David Brittan reports: "Contrary to all expectations, including Meyer's own, neither construction employment nor gross state product—the two measures he used—showed any sign of languishing as a result of the act." Meyer therefore believes that there is much misinformation about the economic impact of the ESA.

Meyer says that the ESA is an easy target for such misinformation, because people are receptive to criticisms about it. Brittan quotes Meyer as saying: "It's hard to be against clean air and water, because people are sensitized to questions of cancer and toxic fumes, and everyone wants to turn on the tap and get clean water. [But the ESA] is an orphan environmental program: the average person doesn't think, 'If this species disappears, my life will change.'"

Threatening a Way of Life

However, according to Brittan, Meyer admits "the possibility that some economic harm could be occurring at the local level." At the same time, he says that anecdotes about individuals harmed by the ESA are often biased. Brittan reports:

> One of the tactics [of ESA opponents] has been to scour the . . . country looking for citizens who say that fish, turtles, or owls have ruined their lives. The trouble is, says Meyer . . . "When I tell you an anecdote, I omit anything that might cloud the picture. But as a scientist, I point out uncertainties in the data, I point out missing information, I point out alternative explanations for why those outcomes

came about." Often, Meyer complains, the anecdotes . . . fall apart under scrutiny.

Meyer believes that most anecdotes about people harmed by the ESA are not true. However, some have been well documented, including the case of Cindy Domenigonis of Riverside County, California, who suffered $400,000 in lost income and regulatory expenses when endangered kangaroo rats were found on her property.

Tom Bethell, in an article in the August 1995 issue of *American Spectator,* reports that as a result of an illegal survey of the Domenigonis farm, the Fish and Wildlife Service discovered the kangaroo rats and ordered the family to set aside eight hundred acres of its farmland. If the family disobeyed the order, the Fish and Wildlife Service would "subject them to a $50,000 fine and/or a year in prison per rat disturbed."

Cindy Domenigonis pleaded with the agency's officials to allow her at least to plow a firebreak on her property. Such firebreaks are necessary in southern California to keep wildfires from spreading.

The Endangered Species Act must protect endangered species such as the kangaroo rat both on private and public lands. One family had to set aside eight hundred acres of farmland when the Fish and Wildlife Service discovered the endangered rodents on their property.

But the Fish and Wildlife Service refused, believing it was protecting the kangaroo rats.

In 1993 a large fire broke out in the area, and without firebreaks it spread out of control. Almost all of the protected kangaroo rat habitat was destroyed, including many surrounding homes.

Cindy Domenigonis's house was saved. But she says she is "no longer pleased to see an eagle, or a hawk or a previously unnoticed flower on our land. Sights like these now cause us great concern that our livelihood and our heritage will be stripped away from us." She considers the ESA a threat not only to her economic well-being but to the safety of her family.

Extreme Measures

Many landowners share this view, and some of them take extreme measures to ensure that endangered species will not hurt their way of life. For example, in the case of the red-cockaded woodpeckers, Benjamin Cone decided to stop the bird from taking up residence in any more of his timber. On the fifty-two hundred acres he still controlled, he began clear-cutting trees at the rate of over three hundred per year, targeting any growth older than forty years. Huge portions of his forest soon became bare land.

Other landowners, like Cone, have discovered that the best way to protect themselves against the ESA is to destroy habitat. As a result, many people believe that the ESA does more harm than good, and should therefore be repealed. In an article in the January 1, 1994, issue of *American Forests*, American Forest Executive Vice President Neil Sampson says:

> The problem [with ESA], it seems to me, goes well beyond the political and economic arguments being hurled back and forth on the issue. ESA today is not only failing in too many instances, it is creating incentives for landowners to actively destroy habitat! When a law designed to protect something results in its destruction, the need for a new approach becomes compelling.

Similarly, economics professor Richard Stroup, in the September 1995 issue of the *American Enterprise*, says:

Many people worry that the Endangered Species Act may encourage further endangerment of species such as the red-cockaded woodpecker. Private citizens who fear government restrictions on their land have cut down forested areas to prevent the settlement of endangered species.

Experiences like Ben Cone's have encouraged landowners around the country to prevent their land from harboring listed species. Some landowners now manage their land in a way that almost assures it will not be suitable for endangered species. Others may even be going to the extreme of [killing and burying an endangered species to hide its presence].

Though there is no proof that people have set out to kill endangered species, there is evidence that the ESA is inadvertently causing their decline. For example, according to Stroup, a 1993 Texas Parks and Wildlife Department report notes that in Texas "more habitat for the black-capped vireo and the golden-checked warbler [birds] has been lost since they were listed under the Endangered Species Act than would have been lost if the ESA had not been applied to them."

Many people, fearing that the same is true for red-cockaded woodpeckers, have proposed economic incentives to keep landowners from destroying woodpecker habitat. For example, an environmental group called the Environmental Defense Fund has suggested offering property tax credits to landowners who leave the birds' pine trees alone. Other groups have recommended government payments to landowners for every endangered species found on their land or for acreage whose use has been restricted.

Richard Stroup believes that incentives, though worthwhile, do not address the basic flaw of the ESA: that it has allowed the government to misuse excessive power to control endangered habitats:

> All these [incentive] approaches are worth considering, but the critical change is to remove the ability of the Fish and Wildlife Service to seize control of land without compensation. . . . Rather than foisting the costs of its programs onto a few unfortunate landowners, the service would be able to take only those actions it could afford, based on funding it received through the normal congressional budget process. This would encourage the service to be more thoughtful and efficient in its executive actions. Once they had to pay for the land they used, the agency staff would begin searching for less intrusive and more cost-effective ways to preserve species.

One such less intrusive approach is already in effect in North Carolina. In his article from the April 1996 issue of *National Wildlife*, Stephen Lipske describes a special program to protect the red-cockaded woodpecker:

> [Under this program, a landowner agrees] to maintain enough pine habitat, as determined by [Fish and Wildlife Service] biologists, to support the four groups of wood-peckers [already] nesting on his land. These groups serve as his baseline birds. If more woodpeckers move onto his land, [the landowner] will not be responsible for protecting the newcomers under the Endangered Species Act, beyond giving biologists time to relocate any affected woodpeckers before he cuts pines.

But relocation programs and other endangered species projects are expensive, and some people believe that the ESA is not worth the cost. One critic is Wallace Kaufman, whose book *No Turning Back: Dismantling the Fantasies of Environmental Thinking,* firmly states that "the Endangered Species Act has not saved any species,

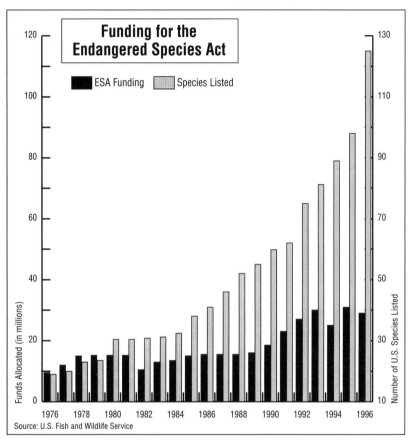

Funding for the Endangered Species Act

■ ESA Funding ▦ Species Listed

Funds Allocated (in millions)

Number of U.S. Species Listed

1976   1978   1980   1982   1984   1986   1988   1990   1992   1994   1996

Source: U.S. Fish and Wildlife Service

[although] the costs for trying have run into the billions." Kaufman supports this opinion by pointing out that since the law was enacted, species have been continually added to the list, but only a few have been removed. If the ESA were effective, he argues, would not there be fewer endangered species on the list each year?

Endangered Successes

It is true that the endangered species list has been growing larger rather than smaller. By 1996 a total of 1,500 domestic and foreign species were listed as endangered, with 243 plants and animals awaiting final approval for addition to the list and another 182 awaiting consideration.

Environmentalists and biologists claim that the increased number of endangered species on the list represents not failure but success:

Biologists are now better funded and so better able to identify endangered species. Environmental groups support research projects throughout the world and investigate species never before identified.

For example, in 1996 several environmental groups, including the Nature Conservancy, BirdLife International, and the World Conservation Monitoring Center, sponsored a comprehensive study on endangered species by the World Conservation Union (IUCN) Species Survival Commission. This study used more than 7,000 scientists, researchers, and environmentalists from 179 countries to catalog 5,205 threatened species worldwide.

Environmentalists also point out that while only seven bird and animal species—including the American alligator, the gray whale, the Arctic peregrine falcon, and the brown pelican—have been removed from the endangered species list, twenty-five are approaching recovery, and 40 percent of the species on the list are stable or improving. By the time a species is listed as endangered, its numbers are so low that environmentalists consider any improvement at all remarkable. As Jeffrey McNeely explains in the March 1992 issue of *Environment* magazine:

To save the endangered whooping crane, the International Crane Foundation raises the birds for release in the wild. Critics of such programs argue that they are unsuccessful in producing enough animals to remove them from the endangered species list.

[When the ESA was created] it contained a political paradox that effectively prevented it from ever working to anyone's satisfaction: A species can receive protection under the act only after its population has been reduced to dangerously low levels, making recovery both costly and inefficient.

Tough Choices

Because of public outcry by property owners affected by the Endangered Species Act, in 1994 the U.S. Congress imposed a moratorium on all its provisions pending its revision. However, President Bill Clinton disagreed with the moratorium and lifted it before the act could be revised.

Nonetheless, many people in Congress continue to criticize the Endangered Species Act. In particular they question whether seemingly insignificant species, such as certain types of insects and fungi, should be added to the list.

In 1991 such invertebrates accounted for 26 percent of the endangered species list. Environmentalists believe that what have been called insignificant creatures and plants deserve as much attention as larger, more popular animals. For example, Valerie Richardson, in the February 13, 1995, issue of the *Washington Times*, quotes Pam Eaton, assistant regional director of the Wilderness Society: "I don't think it's in the best interest to change the act so we can say, 'OK, let's let this species go extinct,' which is what I think [ESA opponents] are talking about."

Environmentalists like Pam Eaton do not want to sacrifice any species, even to benefit another. They believe that because everything on earth is interrelated, maintaining biological diversity is important to the survival of human beings. For example, Professor Stephen Meyer says: "They should never have called it the Endangered Species Act, because that allows a congressperson to say, 'How can saving any one species be worth the trouble.' . . . [But people don't understand.] When you protect [single species like] the spotted owl, you protect the old-growth forest, and when you protect the old-growth forest, you protect the 100 other species in there that you may or may not know about."

Moreover, environmentalists argue that environmental protections should not depend on popularity contests, because apparently worthless species sometimes prove important to human beings. For example, the armadillo was once thought to be an expendable creature. Now, however, researchers have discovered that it helps fight a serious human disease called leprosy. In his book *Save the Earth*, Jonathon Porritt explains: "After injection with diseased cells, tissues from [the armadillo's] spleen and liver are now used in production of an anti-leprosy vaccine."

Porritt says that this discovery means the armadillo is now worth saving. But he adds that this case illustrates the way people judge a creature's worth. He states: "While this is crucially important for leprosy sufferers, it raises difficult questions about how we measure the 'value' of other species. Is the armadillo only considered to be of value because it is of use to us?"

But usefulness is only one criterion by which people judge a species' worth. Attractiveness and uniqueness are two other qualities that influence opinions. According to environmentalist Robert

Since armadillos were recently found to be useful in producing a cure for leprosy, many people no longer view them as expendable animals.

"What have you done for us lately?"

Devine, Americans typically value large or unusual birds and mammals more than lesser ones and consider all vertebrates more important than invertebrates. In the July 1996 issue of *Sierra* magazine, he cites a study wherein "respondents ranked 247 listed species according to perceived importance. Number one was the bald eagle, and the top 10 included other heavy hitters like the grizzly, the whooping crane, and the sea otter. The highest rated mini-organism was the Bay checker spot butterfly, which came in 62nd. The bottom 10 consisted of half a dozen mini-organism plus two rats, a bat, and a snake, with the Kretschmarr Cave mold beetle coming in dead last—perhaps a prophetic phrase."

Devine says that these values influence environmental expenditures. He reports that while an average of only $44,000 of ESA money is currently spent on helping invertebrates, an average of $684,000 is spent on each listed mammal species. He wants more money to be spent on invertebrates.

However, some people believe that no money should be spent on plants or insects. For example, according to Devine, the National Wilderness Institute, a conservative research organization, "wants the nation to abandon the ESA's intent to protect all species, and change it to allow the public's preference for [larger species] to guide the official decision-making process." In other words, the

*Bald eagles have made a remarkable recovery after being on the brink of
extinction. Popular species like the bald eagle receive more support from
both the public and the government than their smaller counterparts.*

ESA would protect only mammals, and all ESA money would be
allotted accordingly.

An Expensive Program

In fact, large species already receive more direct benefits from the
ESA than small ones. For example, among endangered birds, the bald
eagle, the Arctic peregrine falcon, and the brown pelican have
received more donations of time and money from both the environmental community and the federal government than lesser species. As
a result, all three have been removed from the endangered species list.

However, there is a limit to how much people are willing to
spend on even a popular species. For example, when the California
condor was first identified as critically endangered, the American
public rallied to save the bird, which has a dramatic wingspan of
nearly ten feet and can fly 150 miles in one day. However, now that
the total cost of the California Condor Recovery Program (CCRP)
has exceeded $20 million, many people are less enthusiastic about
preservation.

According to Stephanie Simon, the federal government supports the CCRP through taxpayer dollars, which are administered through the offices of the U.S. Fish and Wildlife Service. The program began in 1987, when the last wild California condors were captured and placed under the care of biologists. These fourteen birds were encouraged to breed, and the resulting thirteen chicks were raised to adulthood and released back into the wild in 1992 and 1993.

Five of the thirteen released birds died almost immediately. One was electrocuted on power lines, three slammed into utility poles, and one drank antifreeze, a toxic substance used in automobiles. As a result, the biologists recaptured the remaining birds and took them to the Los Angeles Zoo, where they and subsequent condor offspring are trained to avoid such hazards as power lines and people.

This training program currently costs taxpayers approximately $500,000 a year. Thomas Lambert says that "most Americans are willing to pay taxes . . . to protect beautiful, dramatic, or 'cuddly' species," but others disagree, claiming that the CCRP is too expensive and that condors are not clearly worth saving. Mary F. Pols

The California condor has been the subject of a massive, yet largely unsuccessful, effort to save it from extinction.

quotes one critic: "The condor is not a majestic bird but a common buzzard which lives on road kill. If you think that . . . [anyone] would be excited to see these birds gnawing away on a dead animal carcass along the road you are very mistaken. That is not a pretty sight." However, Pols insists that "after years of [direct contact with condors], most condor watchers admit to finding the legendary birds oddly endearing."

Yet even some condor supporters do not approve of certain aspects of the CCRP. Members of the Sierra Club, for example, have spoken out against training the birds. Mark Palmer of the Sierra Club's national wildlife committee says: "If we're creating these designer condors for the wild and pretending we're back in the good old days with real condors, we're just fooling ourselves."

According to Stephanie Simon, Palmer believes that these "new and improved" condors are not the same as their wild predecessors because they have lost their natural instincts. She says that Palmer dislikes the idea of a "tailor-made vulture" that "might be able to survive in the modern world, but would lack the prehistoric instincts that guided its ancestors millions of years ago, in the era of the woolly mammoth and great ground sloth." Palmer does not want the CCRP to change the behavior of the condors before releasing them, but Simon says: "To biologists, . . . a manipulated condor is better than a dead condor."

Mixing Condor Breeds

Many environmentalists believe that people should do whatever it takes to keep a species from becoming extinct. This philosophy has led some to suggest a new breeding program for California condors. The program would mate California condors with Andean condors, which are not endangered. According to Alston Chase, in his article "Secretive Expansion of Endangered Species Act Not Designed to Save Species," the U.S. Fish and Wildlife Service wants to change the rules of the ESA so that the resulting hybrid chicks would be classified as California condors, providing they look like California condors. This means that a creature resembling an endangered species would be considered endangered, even though its biological classification would differ.

Many people object to this proposed change. They say that adding hybrids to the endangered species list would violate its intent, because scientists would then be inbreeding species into a different kind of extinction. In other words, there would no longer be "pure" California condors on earth. Moreover, these critics believe that the ESA is expensive enough without expanding the endangered species list to include hybrids. Chase reports:

> Many insiders [within the Fish and Wildlife Service] are livid. Not only does hybrid listing encourage biological mischief, it promises virtually limitless expansion of . . . [the Endangered Species Act]. Longtime Wildlife Service employees note that the change virtually renders meaningless all mention of "species" in the Endangered Species Act. . . . And, like mongrel dogs, the variety of "intercrosses" that could be listed is almost limitless. If you thought the 959 creatures currently designated endangered or threatened cause problems, just wait until hybrids flood the scrolls.

Chase also says that many people object to the Fish and Wildlife Service's practice of releasing animals in places other than their native habitats. He reports that in 1995 "the agency was criticized for releasing eight Texas cougars into Florida."

In the case of the California condor, residents of San Juan County, Arizona, filed suit in federal court to stop the release of the birds there in 1996. CCRP scientists had previously released its condors in the mountains north of Los Angeles, but they decided that the Grand Canyon region along the Utah-Arizona border would be a safer place for the birds than southern California.

However, residents of Utah and Arizona objected to the plan. In fact, according to Maggie Farley in the April 28, 1996, edition of the *Los Angeles Times*, they lodged so many angry complaints with public officials that "environmentalists questioned whether the birds would be safe in the hostile country," and eventually the officials went to court to fight the condor release.

Reporter Carey Hamilton explains that the county residents were afraid "that the birds' reintroduction [would] lead to limits on

tourism. . . . The county [was] concerned that if the condors settle in
the Glen Canyon Recreation Area, they would have to be treated as
an endangered species and that would limit commercial activity." In
response to such fears, the federal government guaranteed that the
appearance of the condors would not impact logging, mining, ranching, and other activities in the region.

Consequently, according to Mark Potok, even the most vocal
opponents began to accept reintroduction. He quotes antirelease
activist Joy Jordan: "People in this area have no problem with trying to save an endangered species. We just don't like to have it
crammed down our throats. But now I'm feeling very good [about
federal officials]. They were willing to negotiate and listen to our
problems." As a result, on December 12, 1996, biologists were
allowed to release six young condors in Arizona. Five are still alive;
the sixth was killed by a golden eagle a month after its release.

Property Rights

In the case of the California condors, the federal government worked
with residents to allay their economic concerns, promising to limit
certain aspects of ESA enforcement so local businesses would not be
hurt. This waiver ultimately benefited their environmental program.
But in other cases, environmentalists argue that the only way to protect the environment is to have stricter ESA enforcement.

In particular, environmentalists want to restrict property rights so
that landowners cannot do whatever they want with their own land.
They believe that without stricter government regulations, endangered
habitats will be destroyed as developers build malls and housing tracts
without considering their environmental impact. In the days before
the ESA, such habitat destruction did occur, and many animals in the
United States were hunted to near extinction. Environmentalists
believe that these practices would resume if the ESA is abolished, and
they want the ESA strengthened rather than weakened.

But opponents object to this idea. For example, Wallace Kaufman, in his book *No Turning Back*, says that the government should
not ignore property rights in the name of environmentalism. He and
other critics want the Endangered Species Act repealed or modified
to allow landowners more control over the use of their own property.

This blue heron is very susceptible to the effects of pollution in its wetland environment. Such interconnectedness among species and their habitats has led to increased regulations to protect the environment.

Arguments over repeal of the ESA resemble those over the government's ability to control America's national parks. Both debates involve costs, benefits, and property rights, and both hinge on one difficult question: Can private citizens and corporations be trusted to care for America's important wilderness areas?

Chapter 2

How Should America's Federal Wilderness Areas Be Managed?

IN JANUARY 1997 A MAJOR storm hit California's Yosemite National Park, and the Merced River overflowed, washing away campsites and permanent installations. In some places, the water rose six to eight feet. Its force felled trees and broke pipes in the park's new sewer system, and Yosemite was closed to visitors.

Seventy-three days later the park reopened, but it was not the same. The storm not only destroyed Yosemite's sewer system but damaged much of the famous attraction's infrastructure, including buildings, roads, and bridges. Park officials estimate that the cost of replacing these damaged structures could exceed $178 million. One road alone, a 7.5-mile section of Highway 140 that leads to one of Yosemite's entrances, might cost more than $18 million.

Under the current system, this expense would be met with federal funds. According to a report in the February 7, 1997, issue of *USA Today*, the federal budget allocated $23 billion for natural resources and the environment in 1997. But this money must fund all of the more than 370 entities in the national park system, which is managed by the National Park Service, as well as the approximately 192 million acres of national forests managed by the U.S. Forest Service. All of these wilderness areas compete for the same limited dollars.

Therefore, some people question whether Yosemite is entitled to such a large share of federal wilderness funds. Federal officials have responded to this criticism by proposing special legislation to

Thirty-foot sections of asphalt were uprooted by the flood that devastated Yosemite National Park in 1997.

finance repairs on three major roads and some of the campgrounds and trails with nonwilderness federal dollars. But this means that the government would have to reduce funding for other budget items, such as defense, in order to pay for Yosemite.

Meanwhile, the estimated cost of repairs in Yosemite is rising, because environmentalists want many of the park's tourist facilities rebuilt in different locations. According to an article in the March 10, 1997, issue of *Newsday:*

Visitors view the magnificent scenes from Glacier Point at Yosemite
National Park. One of the most heavily used of the national parks,
Yosemite's traffic is a cause for debate between tourists, who want the
park to rebuild its campgrounds, and environmentalists, who think that
the park is overused and want to reduce tourism.

> Many who love [Yosemite] view [the flood] as a once-in-a-lifetime chance to undo much of what is "wrong" with this immensely popular national park. . . . If Congress grants the millions and the Clinton administration has the political will, federal officials say, they want to turn parking lots back into meadows, push campgrounds away from the river, move housing . . . and offices out of the crowded valley and attempt to get people out of their automobiles and onto shuttle buses—or even walking.

Tim Golden reports that the park's chief of maintenance and engineering, R. Kevin Cann, has estimated that "the changes being proposed . . . would cost about four times as much as simply rebuilding the damaged structures and roads as they were before."

But despite their cost, environmentalists believe such changes are necessary. They argue that man-made structures interfere with people's enjoyment of the park; the best view of Yosemite Falls, for example, is from a parking lot. Such arguments have already persuaded the government to adopt some of the environmentalists' proposed changes.

According to park superintendent B. J. Griffin in Eric Brazil's March 15, 1997, *Los Angeles Daily News* article, the campgrounds beside the Merced River will not be rebuilt. Moreover, Griffin says that returning visitors will find Yosemite "a different and more natural experience," adding that in the future, "the human footprint will be smaller" in the park. In other words, there will be fewer tourist facilities in Yosemite than before.

Environmentalist Jay Thomas Watson, the western regional director of the Wilderness Society, applauds this change. In a March 12, 1997, letter to *USA Today,* he says that he hopes his children "will remember [Yosemite] for its granite cliffs, blue sky and silence more than for asphalt . . . and souvenir shops." He wants the park restored to its "natural character."

Similarly, Paul C. Pritchard, president of the National Parks and Conservation Association, believes that America's wilderness areas need to be safeguarded from human destruction. In a February 2, 1997, US Newswire article, he states:

Our ultimate goal is to make sure that our national parks are healthy and intact when we pass them along to future generations. But for that to happen, we must first have a full understanding of the natural and cultural treasures that make up the parks. It's not just the animals and plants, it's microorganisms and fossil records. It's archaeological sites and historic buildings. It's everything that makes the parks unique places.

Pritchard wants the federal government to allocate more national park funds for scientific research and less for tourist facilities. But others disagree with his priorities. As Golden explains, "The flood [in Yosemite] has . . . propelled the country's busiest national park back to the center of a long and quickening national debate over how the Park Service should balance its often contradictory mandates. The agency is supposed to preserve the environmental quality of the national parks, but it is obliged to keep them accessible to tourists at the same time."

Garner B. Hanson, in a March 10, 1997, editorial in *USA Today*, argues that tourists should be the first concern of the National Park Service. In the case of Yosemite, he says,

It is shortsighted for . . . the National Park Service to leap on the tragedy at Yosemite as an opportunity for a "scouring action" leading to many restrictions on the people's right to visit, use, and enjoy a park that has been acquired, maintained and paid for by the partnership of the U.S. taxpayers and the private-sector [businesses that operate inside the parks] over the past years.

Hanson sees no reason to decrease tourist facilities, because "all roads and visitor services in our parks take up only about 1% of the land area, with nearly all the rest being preserved in its natural state." He also opposes plans to limit tourist visits to Yosemite.

Environmentalists have proposed cutting the number of summer visitors allowed into Yosemite from 17,000 people a day to 10,500, and the number of overnight guests from 9,000 to 7,700; the park currently receives over 1 million visitors a year, more than any other national park. But Hanson argues that with careful planning, "even more visitors can enjoy our parks without endangering the resources." He says that Americans should "not turn back the clock and discourage people from using and enjoying their national parks because the government can't plan creatively to accommodate them."

Hanson's position is part of an ongoing debate over the management of America's federal wilderness areas. This debate centers around two questions: Who should benefit from these lands, and who should pay for their management?

Fund-Raising Efforts

Critics of America's wilderness system argue that the United States can no longer afford to maintain so many acres of public property. Some have suggested that management of national parks and forests therefore be turned over to state or local governments.

In a May 1996 *World & I* article, Terry Anderson suggests that state agencies are better able to pay for individual wilderness areas, because, unlike their federal counterparts, they have the power to fund conservation programs through local events. Anderson, a professor of economics at Montana State University who has written about the economic impact of environmentalism, explains:

> In Texas, [state] park managers generate revenues from dances, weddings, bird-watching tours, nature seminars, and "Christmas in the parks." On just 500,000 acres, one-fourth the area of Yellowstone [National Park], Texas parks generate $25 million annually, compared with Yellowstone's $3 million.

Anderson also criticizes the federal government for not trying harder to make America's national parks self-supporting. In particular, he says that entrance fees to national parks are far too low, considering the cost of maintaining a park. For example, in 1993 each visitor to Yellowstone Park cost taxpayers approximately $4.70, because the average admission fee per person was only $1.30 while operating costs were $6 per person. Anderson explains: "Yellowstone, the 'crown jewel' of our park system, has 2.2 million acres

The Texas Park Service's innovative fund-raising techniques have allowed the state to raise eight times the revenue of Yellowstone National Park, even though parks like Big Bend (pictured) are used much less.

and 3 million visitors. Yet its budget for operations is only $17 million, shameful for a park of its size, and its backlog of capital improvements exceeds $250 million."

Anderson points out that when the National Park Service was created in 1917, it was entirely funded by visitor fees. But as entrance fees remained the same while costs rose, the service came to rely more and more on government funding. Anderson says: "To make the park experience better for visitors, we need to raise fees and allow managers to use those fees for improving visitor services."

However, the federal government is currently trying to address this problem. In 1997 it raised entrance fees at many national parks, including the Grand Canyon, the Grand Tetons, Yosemite, and Yellowstone. In announcing the upcoming fee hike on November 26, 1996, Interior Secretary Bruce Babbit said: "While everything else has gone up in price over the past 70 years, Yellowstone is still $10 per car. That's less than the price of a good video of the park, and much less than it costs to visit an amusement park in Florida." Senator Slade Gorton of Washington State added: "Tax dollars alone can no longer fully satisfy the demand for increased recreation opportunities and facilities."

According to Cathy Lynn Grossman, in a March 14, 1997, *USA Today* article, the government's fee increases "are expected to raise $140 million for maintenance and capital improvements on federal lands by the year 2000." National Park Service director Roger Kennedy believes that this money is necessary to maintain America's wilderness areas. In a March 13, 1997, *Newsday* article by Bill Bleyer, Kennedy says that the increase in revenue "will provide needed funds to begin fixing the badly deteriorated infrastructure of our aging parks system." Kennedy estimates that the parks currently need $5.6 billion worth of repairs and maintenance.

Because so much money is needed, some people believe that the new entrance fees ($2 per person without a vehicle or $20 per car), are still too low, particularly in comparison to what other private recreational activities cost. For example, according to Kevin McNamee, in his September 1, 1996, *Nature Canada* article "Pay Per View," the superintendent of Glacier National Park told a *New York Times* reporter: "To get into a water slide just outside the park costs $7.50—that's 50 percent more than it costs for a carload to get into Glacier Park for 10 days."

Rangers at Yosemite National Park accept entrance fees from visitors eager to tour the park. Raising such entrance fees may be one solution to raising more money for park maintenance.

McNamee says that Canada, which has the world's oldest national park service, is facing the same park financing problems as the United States. It has decided to increase revenues by raising its fees based on personal benefit. He explains:

> Canada's basic financial principle is that tax dollars pay for the cost of having and protecting national parks and national historic sites. Thus, taxpayers will pay for those park values that benefit society as a whole, including the preservation of more wilderness and wildlife habitat, the maintenance of ecological services such as clean air and water, and the provision of educational programs.

> Conversely, park visitors who personally benefit from the use of park facilities will pay for them through increased fees. The rationale is that taxpayers should not subsidize individuals who derive a private benefit—such as the use of campgrounds—from their stay in a park.

Canada's park service charges park visitors increased fees to tour its national parks. Such fees are applied to park upkeep.

Many people believe that this principle should be applied to all U.S. wilderness areas. For example, Philip Brasher, in his January 26, 1997, *Los Angeles Times* article "Forest Service Fees Too Low," reports:

> Looking for a vacation bargain? Try a lakefront cabin in a national forest. A lot along Minnesota's Lake Winnibigoshish can be had for a fee of $355 a year, less than a third of what it should be, according to congressional auditors who say people are being charged too little to use national forests.

Brasher says that many people believe that the federal government charges far too little for the use of its wilderness areas. He quotes Jerome Uher, a spokesman for the National Parks and Conservation Association: "You see across the board the charges that the government imposes are usually much lower than what you're going to see from the private sector or even state governments."

Yet even some environmentalists object to an increase in national park fees. For example, in a February 19, 1997, *Los Angeles Times* article, Nicholas Riccardi reports that the Sierra Club has objected to charging a $5 daily parking fee for people who use the Angeles National Forest in southern California, even though that money will go directly towards $20 million in park maintenance projects. He quotes one Sierra Club member, Fred Hoeptner, as saying that although the amount seems "reasonable . . . you don't know if it will stay that way in the future."

The Sierra Club suggests that instead of charging people to use national parks, which are already funded by public tax dollars, the government should be charging private companies more to use park resources. Riccardi explains that according to Hoeptner, "some [Sierra Club] members have complained that the Angeles National Forest undercharges television companies for their placement of antennas atop Mt. Wilson [within park boundaries], and that those fees should be raised before visitors have to pay."

Privatization

However, many people believe that increasing entrance or user fees will not solve the current money crisis within the federal wilderness system. Some have suggested that the only solution is for the government to yield public-sector responsibility for the land. For example, in a December 1996 *Society* article, Robert Nelson, a professor at the School of Public Affairs of the University of Maryland, says that the government should consider selling some of its wilderness areas to private buyers. Ownership could be transferred to individuals or corporations screened to assure that the "wilderness" aspects of the property would be maintained.

Nelson particularly favors selling some of America's federal lands to timber companies. The government currently leases land to such companies, giving them logging rights on a property but not allowing them to own it. But Nelson advocates selling rather than leasing the land because "the operative principle in the American economic system is that if the goal is production for income-earning purposes, the ownership should be in the private sector." He says that "private companies that need to make a profit should be insulated from political interference . . . and freer to operate outside rigid government . . . rules."

Nelson says that there are many ways these land sales could be handled:

> Sale of the lands by competitive bid is one option. A better approach might be to create one or more new corporations and then sell stock in them. Some of the shares could be given to state and local governments that now receive a significant part of the revenue . . . from [the current leasing of] federal timber lands.

Nelson concludes that the "sale of selected areas of national forests would bring in substantial current revenues to the federal government and provide the security of [property ownership] necessary for the private sector to make large long-term investments." But other people strongly object to selling America's wilderness areas, no matter what the economic benefits. For example, Melanie Griffin, in a May 1996 *World & I* article, says:

> Most Americans cannot conceive of selling off our national park lands. And it's no wonder. Our national parks represent the heart of our nation's proud tradition of protecting spe-

cial places for our children and grandchildren. Since the establishment of Yellowstone as the world's first national park in 1872, America's park system has come to represent the best of our natural and cultural heritage.

Griffin does not believe that national parks need to be self-supporting. She believes that economics should not be a part of a discussion on federal wilderness areas. She says:

> No one but the politicians in Washington, D.C., could come up with the idea that our national park system is too large or too expensive. As the *Seattle Post-Intelligencer* editorialized, "The idea, it appears on the surface, is to make the park system pay for itself. That will never happen. It was never intended to happen. The United States' national parks are its crown jewels, held in trust by the government. The parks belong to each citizen."

Whether the National Park Service can adequately manage the nation's parks, such as Glacier National Park (pictured) in Montana, is a subject of debate.

Moreover, Griffin does not trust corporations to behave responsibly towards wilderness areas. She says they have already abused this land as lessees with rights to log, mine, or drill for oil in national forests. She says: "American taxpayers spend billions every year to subsidize environmental destruction caused by multinational mining companies, agribusiness, and large corporate timber interests."

Griffin adds that as concessions to timber companies, the government has spent federal funds on "the construction of new logging roads. Thousands of miles of taxpayer-funded roads are being built in our national forests every year, causing extreme soil erosion, water pollution, and reduced fishing opportunities." She similarly criticizes ranchers' use of federal lands for cattle grazing, saying: "Subsidized livestock grazing on public lands managed by the [Bureau of Land Management] and the Forest Service leads to overgrazing and severe habitat destruction on fragile western lands. According to the Competitive Enterprise Institute, the full cost of BLM grazing management programs, not including Forest Service costs, is $200 million each year."

Griffin believes that if the government charged users for such services, it would not need to sell federal lands. There would be enough revenue to continue to support public wilderness areas under the present system.

But others argue that the government is currently entrusted with more land than it can handle. According to Ken Miller, managing this land is an overwhelming responsibility:

> The Park Service is trying to cope with an increased load as Congress creates new parks, monuments, memorials and other units. Meanwhile, the agency must spend increasing amounts of its thinning budget to comply with more than 20 federal laws, from the Clean Air and Clean Water acts to worker safety, endangered species and toxic-cleanup laws, and requirements to make parks more accessible to disabled visitors.

Nonprofit Groups vs. Corporations

Supporters of privatization believe that the federal government can no longer handle these responsibilities. However, some of them do not define privatization to mean that the land must be sold. Instead, they argue that the government could retain legal ownership of its wilderness areas while still giving private companies all rights and responsibilities regarding the property.

For example, in his book *Playing God in Yellowstone*, Alston Chase reports that many people "advocate turning management of the national parks over to private, nonprofit wilderness endowment boards, organized like art or history museums, but accountable to Congress." Like private museums, these boards would be supported wholly by public donations and user fees, and would rely heavily on volunteer staff. They would therefore be immune to politics and budgetary whims.

Chase believes this kind of privatization would solve the problem of accountability. Under the current system, he maintains, no one really takes responsibility for the individual needs of each wilderness area. He quotes Jane Shaw of the Political Economy Research Center (PERC), which has been studying the privatization of public lands: "When everyone owns a resource, such as air and water, no one actually owns it—and no one is accountable for treating it properly."

However, some people believe that the best organization to run America's wilderness areas is not a nonprofit group but a corporation. Corporations already donate money to the national park system and sponsor individual park projects. Some politicians want to allow them to sponsor entire parks in exchange for advertising.

Harry Blauvelt, in a September 19, 1996, *USA Today* article, reports that the annual revenue from such sponsorships might be as much as $100 million, and Linda Kanamine, also in *USA Today,* says that the National Park Service has proposed a specific program to help garner this revenue. She reports that the service wants the government to "establish an elite cadre of 10 or so sponsors that would give $8 million to $10 million a year each [for park maintenance, repairs, and scientific research]. . . . In return, the sponsors would be able to bill themselves in advertising as exclusive partners of national parks."

But Kanamine also says that this proposal has met with heavy opposition from people who believe that "companies will have basic expectations if they become park sponsors: a recognized logo as exclusive industry sponsor; the right to be the only brand of their product sold within the parks; and recognition on signs or pamphlets of the contribution." Paul Pritchard, of the National Parks and Conservation

Association, responds: "This is one step closer to having 'The Grand Canyon brought to you by Marriott [a hotel chain]' or whoever."

Similarly, Melanie Griffin argues that politicians want to allow corporations not only to sponsor national parks but to run them. She says these politicians "seek to give large corporate interests supremacy over the public lands."

In fact, portions of America's national parks are already privately managed. Their shops, restaurants, and other profitable concerns are run not by the government but by concessionaires. Concessionaires are businesses or individuals who pay a fee for the privilege of running a private business within a public facility.

Yosemite's concessionaire is the Delaware North Company, which was given the right to operate ski lifts, shops, restaurants, hotels, and other profit-oriented concerns within the park. In return it must pay the government $25 of every $100 in profit. A share of this money—4.5 percent of all gross profits, or approximately $4 million out of the $90 million the company earns yearly—goes directly into a special fund for park improvements.

As of 1996, $9.6 million had been placed into this fund, earmarked only for Yosemite. In addition, Delaware North had completed twenty-one improvement projects at a cost of $2.1 million, and was planning to build a 150-seat amphitheater.

However, this arrangement is unusual. While most concessions in national parks are privately run, they typically contribute much less money directly to a park. As of 1996, 744 concessionaires in 132 parks paid only 2 percent or less of their profits to the federal treasury. In 1993, this meant that of $657 million in sales, the concessionaires paid the government only $17.7 million.

Many people therefore believe that without strict controls, private corporations will always choose to increase profits rather than contribute to a park's maintenance. They fear that if corporations ran every aspect of America's wilderness areas, similar neglect would occur. For example, Griffin fears that corporate privatization would mean "the exploitation of oil and minerals on every possible national wildlife refuge, and national forests clearcut at an accelerated rate."

But supporters of corporate privatization believe that private companies would want to protect these lucrative tourist attractions.

Ahwahnee Hotel in Yosemite National Park is run by a private commercial company that must give part of its profits to the National Park Service.

Chase quotes Terry Anderson: "I have no problem with the idea of the Disney people running Yellowstone." Such people believe that amusement park operators have the expertise necessary to manage the large volume of visitors that America's national parks attract.

Different Standards

But opponents of privatization say that even the most reputable and well-intentioned companies will apply different standards to the job of managing America's national parks than the National Park Service does. Corporations will not only make their decisions based on a desire to increase profits but limit activities and alter features within the parks to minimize risk and avoid expensive lawsuits. Maureen West, writing about a July 1996 rock slide in Yosemite that killed one person and injured twelve, says:

> If [Yosemite] were Disneyland, when an unthinking reporter asked a park spokesman what he was going to do

to prevent future rock slides, the answer might have been something like: "Bolt down those rocks." Instead, since this was no theme park, [a ranger] said the national park could do nothing to prevent future natural disasters. Rock slides happen every day at Yosemite.

Most people agree that privatizing America's federal wilderness areas will change the way they are managed. However, they disagree on whether these changes would be good or bad. Garner Hanson believes the current system is still viable, pointing out that "the founders of our present-day National Park system envisioned a partnership between the park service and its private-sector concessioners which would welcome visitors to these special places."

But others believe that the federal government can no longer afford its wilderness areas. Some accuse the government of mismanaging its national parks and forests by promoting tourism over preservation of delicate natural resources, and others accuse the government of not exploiting those natural resources aggressively enough. Thus the debate over who should pay for and benefit from federal lands continues.

Chapter 3

Is America's Garbage Really a Problem?

BY JANUARY 1, 2002, the Fresh Kills landfill on Staten Island, in New York Bay, must shut down due to a new state law. New Yorkers currently dump thirteen thousand tons of household trash per day on the island. What will happen to their garbage once the landfill closes?

In an article in the November 4, 1996, issue of *Newsday*, Michele Salcedo explains that this question is so far unanswered. She quotes Manhattan councilman Stanley Michels: "You can't dump [the trash] in the ocean, and incineration has had its day in this city. We have to cut down on the waste stream. We have to increase recycling, we have to do composting, we have to do waste prevention with less packaging. And we're going to have to do a certain amount of exporting."

By "exporting," Councilman Michels means shipping New York's garbage elsewhere. The estimated cost of distant disposal is over $200 million per year, more than twice the cost of running the Fresh Kills landfill, and it is uncertain whether enough other jurisdictions would be willing to accept the exported trash, even for a fee. In 1987, a garbage barge carrying trash from Long Island, New York, was rejected by five states before finding a dump site.

However, a city task force studying the Fresh Kills closure believes that it will find private companies willing to receive tons of trash from New York City. In fact, the task force negotiated a contract with one county in Virginia to take seventeen hundred tons of trash a day. It also issued a plan for trash exportation, and another study has identified over two hundred square miles of possible landfill sites throughout the state. These landfills would offer enough space to solve New York's trash disposal problems for the next 180 years.

But many people have criticized the task force and other public officials for neglecting recycling as a solution to New York City's trash problem. Currently, the city has a recycling rate of only 14 percent of its total trash, compared with over 33 percent in Los Angeles and 48 percent in Seattle. Moreover, in 1996 New York City's mayor, Rudolph Giuliani, cut funding for the city's recycling program by 40 percent, from $69 million to $42 million, which meant fewer curbside pickups.

Landfill Controversies

New York City's trash problems are similar to those of other large cities throughout the nation, where landfills are a common but unsatisfactory way to deal with garbage. For example, Los Angeles County currently disposes of over 300,000 tons of waste per week, and experts have estimated that this amount will increase more than 21 percent by the year 2010. At that time, the county will have to find a way to dispose of more than 150,000 tons of waste per week beyond what existing landfills can handle. Officials have proposed the creation of new landfills, but so far the public has been fighting the idea.

In many parts of the country, people already living near landfills can testify to the unpleasant results. Salcedo offers this graphic description of the Fresh Kills landfill:

Waste Generation and Recovery Practices, 1960–2000

	1960	1970	1980	1990	1994	2000 (projected)
Generation	2.67	3.29	3.67	4.33	4.40	4.42
Recovery for recycling/composting	0.17	0.21	0.35	1.04	0.72	1.33
Discards after recovery	2.50	3.08	3.33	3.61	3.36	3.09
Combustion	0.82	0.67	0.88	0.70	0.68	0.67
Discards to landfill	1.66	2.40	3.00	2.91	2.68	2.42
Population (in millions)	180.00	204.00	227.30	249.40	260.30	276.20

Source: National Solid Waste Management Association   ☐ Pounds per person per day

The Fresh Kills landfill on Staten Island is 4.6 square miles of rotting food, dirty diapers, broken appliances and other discards. It's swarming with seagulls, belching pollution into the air and water, and stinking so bad that shoppers at a nearby mall hold their noses and sprint from car to store.

Consequently, people tend to object when they hear that a new landfill might be opened in their community. They protest offensive odors as well as the landfill's potential to become an environmental and human

Fresh Kills landfill on Staten Island, New York, is piled so high with garbage that when it closes in 2005, it will be taller and heavier than Khufu's pyramid in Egypt.

health hazard. Many older landfills have contaminated their surroundings; for example, experts recently discovered that Los Angeles County's second largest landfill, Puente Hills, has been leaking harmful materials into the groundwater for years.

The Fresh Kills landfill has also polluted area waters. Salcedo reports that the facility "would never be permitted today" because "it was built on a tidal wetland . . . and it's unlined, meaning the ground absorbs all runoff." The Environmental Defense Fund (EDF) reports that such problems are common, given the number of outdated landfills.

Because of pollution problems, many of these outdated landfills can no longer accept new trash. Between 1978 and 1988, the number of operating landfills fell from 14,000 to 5,500. But the EDF maintains that pollution problems are not relegated strictly to older landfills, and that even modern landfills will eventually harm the environment:

> Even the best-designed landfills suffer inherent deficiencies. All of the structures built into the landfill to contain the waste—liners, leachate collection systems, and final cover materials—have finite lifetimes, whereas the wastes and their toxic emissions will continue to exist for decades or longer.

THE WASTE DISPOSAL SOLUTION OF THE
FUTURE: PERSONAL IN-HOME LAND-FILLS

However, analysts disagree. Some argue that landfills are neither as harmful nor as scarce as environmentalists suggest. For example, in the June 30, 1996, issue of the *New York Times Magazine,* reporter John Tierney says:

> America today has a good deal more landfill space available [now] than it did 10 years ago. Landfills are scarce in just a few places, notably the Northeast, partly because of local economic realities (open land is expensive near cities) but mainly because of local politics. Environmentalists have prevented new landfills from opening by propounding [the] myth [that our] garbage will poison us. . . .
>
> Today's landfills for municipal trash are filled mostly with innocuous materials like paper, yard waste and construction debris. They contain small amounts of hazardous wastes, like lead and mercury, but studies have found that these poisons stay trapped inside the mass of garbage even in the old, unlined dumps that were built before today's stringent regulations. So there's little reason to worry about modern landfills, which by Federal law must be lined with clay and plastic, equipped with drainage and gas-collection systems, covered daily with soil and monitored regularly for underground leaks.

Wallace Kaufman, in *No Turning Back*, agrees that landfills are harmless. He believes that the trash issue is not based on public health: "The problem is more economic and psychological. Who wants to live near a dump? And how much will we have to pay to haul garbage to a dump site?"

Incineration

With so much public protest over landfills, what are the alternatives? In some places, one is incineration. For example, the city of Paris, France, has no trash dumps. It burns all its garbage in three incinerators. This process decreases the weight of the trash by 85 percent and its volume to 5 percent of its original size. It also produces heat, which the city captures and then uses to warm some of its public buildings.

French officials are pleased by this beneficial by-product of incineration. "In France we consider the most important thing is to get value out of garbage," says Francis Chalot of France's Environment Ministry, according to Christopher Burns in the February 5, 1995, *Los Angeles Times*.

In other cities, incinerators are used to produce electricity. Roger Starr in the September 1991 issue of *Public Interest*, explains:

> Incineration in high-temperature . . . incinerators uses heat produced by the burning of waste to produce steam that, in turn, generates electricity. This technology is used successfully in many parts of the United States. In Bridgeport, Connecticut, such an incinerator-cum-electric-generator produces 10 percent of the electric power. . . . The incinerator produces no smoke because of the high temperatures used in its burning process. It has been pronounced safe by Connecticut regulatory authorities and has been in operation for several years. There are no odors in the neighborhood of the plant. The residue of the burning consists of ash, amounting to about 10 percent of the volume of the incinerated wastes. The ash is buried in a sanitary landfill.

But many people do not agree with this safe portrayal of incineration. Burns quotes a study by the environmental group Greenpeace that states that waste incineration "threatens to become the leading contributor to the degradation of human and environmental health." According to Greenpeace, the process of incineration produces toxic chemicals such as dioxin, which can cause cancer and birth defects.

According to Bill Breen in the March 1991 issue of *Garbage* magazine, incineration does produce worrisome types of air pollution:

> If municipal solid waste consisted only of carbon and hydrogen, then complete combustion would yield only carbon dioxide and water. However, the garbage stream includes leaves and vegetables, releasing nitrogen oxide when burned; dyes and paints, releasing hydrogen chloride; household batteries, releasing lead; and insecticides and

A typical garbage incinerator in Brooklyn, New York. Mass burning furnaces are the most common type of incinerator used in the United States. The diagram below gives an overview of the way such an incinerator works.

The Incinerator Process

Preparation

1. Trucks unload trash into an enclosed storage pit.

2. An overhead crane picks up trash and dumps it down to the furnace.

Burning

3. In the furnace, trash falls on a grate above the flames.

4. While the grate moves around to allow even burning, the garbage is exposed to at least 2000° F for one second.

5. Air is injected above the fire to maintain temperatures of at least 1500° for 15 seconds to destroy dangerous gases.

Energy Production

6. The burning trash and hot air heats water in the boiler to generate steam.

7. The steam drives a turbine to generate electricity.

Aftermath

8. A fan blows leftover gases from the boiler through the scrubber, an air pollution control device.

9. The ashes are removed from the furnace and cooled, and usually are deposited in a landfill.

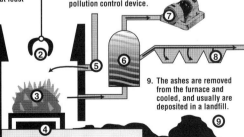

fungicides, releasing arsenic and mercury. What's more, combustion is never complete, and new substances can be formed during burning. . . . [For example,] trace amounts of dioxin arrive [at the incineration plant] in bleached-paper products such as coffee filters, sanitary napkins, and milk containers, and modern garbage burners are extremely efficient at destroying them. So why do tests reveal dioxin in the flue exhaust from incinerators? Some researchers suspect that dioxin reformulates when the gases released by burning garbage cool and attach to particulates [soot and other solid substances] as they fly up the [incinerator] stack.

Breen concedes that older incinerators have been high polluters, but says new incinerators are built to cut down on toxic emissions: "As plants put a lid on their air emissions, much of the dioxin, lead, and cadmium that once flew up the stack now fall down the ash chute. Scrubbers, fabric filters, . . . and other controls are doing a better job of capturing air pollutants."

But according to Breen, this means that "the soot and ash that's left after burning is concentrated with even higher levels of trace metals and organic compounds." Consequently, "the 5.3 million tons of ash which is annually generated by incinerators is a harvest no one wants."

Recycling Programs

Another solution offered in the garbage problem is to decrease the production of materials thrown away, thereby reducing the need for more landfills and incinerators. For example, Bob Collins of the environmental group Clean Water Action says: "Instead of taking years and spending millions to build a major incinerator, why not use the same amount of resources to work our way past the 40 percent recycling level?"

Environmental groups such as the Environmental Defense Fund promote recycling as more than just a way to reduce trash. The EDF says that recycling "helps individuals solve environmental problems in their daily lives," and Roger Starr, in the April 1995 issue of *Public Interest*, explains:

The recycling process is given top priority by the environmental organizations and their followers because it involves the citizenry as a whole in a daily or weekly reminder of the importance of environmental protection. Recycling, the organizations insist, enlivens public consciousness and opens new vistas of public participation in the agenda of environmentalism.

In addition, the EDF insists that separate collection programs for recyclables have economic benefits: "The curbside recycling program diverts material that would otherwise have to be picked up by the regular collection service. Cost savings result because the regular trucks do not have to be unloaded as frequently, and regular collection routes consequently can be rearranged for greater efficiency."

Tierney also admits that recycling has its benefits; for example, "researchers have concluded that recycling does at least save energy—the extra fuel burned while picking up recyclables is more than offset by the energy savings from manufacturing less virgin paper, glass, and metal."

Cities across the country have implemented mandatory waste recycling programs. Critics argue that such programs are unnecessary.

But as a comparison of New York City recycling rates with those of Seattle shows, public participation can vary greatly. There is a 34 percent difference in the recycling rates of those two cities, prompting many environmentalists to suggest that we improve recycling rates by making all recycling programs mandatory, with severe economic penalties for noncooperation.

Some communities have already done this. In Philadelphia, for example, commercial property owners must follow strict recycling guidelines. If these guidelines are violated, businesses can be issued notices of violation and fined up to $300 for every day of noncompliance.

Joseph Bast is the president of the Heartland Institute, a nonprofit research organization in Illinois that studies social problems. He believes that recycling, though a worthwhile activity, is not essential:

Volunteers run a recycling station in their neighborhood.

A lot of people recycle because they're afraid that we're running out of renewable or non-renewable resources—and we know that that isn't true. We've got plenty of trees. We keep discovering new reserves of copper. In the Northeast, landfill space is at a premium. It's still a lot cheaper in New York to landfill than it is to recycle. And incinerators are safe, too. You're exposed to more potentially carcinogenic compounds in one cup of coffee than you are from an entire year of exposure to incinerator fumes.

Another objection to mandatory recycling is that it may produce a glut of recyclables that simply will not be used. If more garbage is collected than sold, then recyclers are faced with a serious problem. As Bill Brown explains in *USA Today Magazine:* "We lose money on recycling."

Brown is the director of environmental affairs at waste management giant WMX Technologies, the world's largest hauler and recycler of solid waste. He says: "It costs $150–200 a ton to collect from the curbside and sort household refuse. We might make $40 a ton from selling waste materials, and we might avoid $30 a ton of landfill charges. But [the] bottom line is that it's not profitable."

Waste management companies offset these losses by charging trash pickup fees. Tierney supports such fees, believing that they make recycling cost-effective. He particularly supports making individuals rather than communities pay the fees. In this "pay-as-you-go" system, people are responsible for the trash they themselves generate. Tierney explains:

> Your trash is already your private property. You should . . . have to pay to get rid of it—and you should pay whatever it takes to ensure that your garbage doesn't cause environmental problems for anyone else. Paying for residential garbage collection sounds like a radical idea in . . . cities where these costs are hidden in property taxes, but it's already being done in thousands of communities. . . . Some cities charge according to volume—the number of bags or cans that you fill—and some have begun experimenting with charging by the pound. Once people switch to this pay-

as-you-throw system, they throw away less—typically at least 10 to 15 percent less.

The Benefits of Recycling

Tierney criticizes environmental groups for failing to promote pay-as-you-go systems as aggressively as they support recycling programs. He accuses environmentalists of favoring recycling not because it benefits the environment but because it benefits their own wallets:

> The leaders of the recycling movement derive psychic and financial rewards from recycling. Environmental groups raise money and attract new members through their campaigns to

Trash cans are separated into different recyclable items. Some states fine individuals and businesses who do not cooperate with such mass recycling programs.

outlaw "waste" and prevent landfills from opening. They get financing from public and private sources (including the recycling industry) to research and promote recycling. By turning garbage into a political issue, environmentalists have created jobs for themselves as lawyers, lobbyists, researchers, educators and moral guardians.

Tierney questions whether recycling really benefits the environment. He says that in the case of newspapers, for example, recycling might actually do more harm to the environment than cutting down trees:

> Saving a tree is a mixed blessing. When there's less demand for virgin wood pulp, timber companies are likely to sell some of their tree farms—maybe to condominium developers. Less virgin pulp means less pollution at paper mills in timber country, but recycling operations create pollution in areas where more people are affected: fumes and noise from collection trucks, solid waste and sludge from the mills that remove ink and turn the paper into pulp. Recycling newspaper actually creates more water pollution than making new paper: for each ton of recycled newsprint that's produced, an extra 5,000 gallons of waste water are discharged.

Wallace Kaufman also believes that recycling is not economically practical:

> As most homeowners know, it is cheaper to buy a new piece of lumber than to hire someone to tear down a building and sort, denail, and trim old lumber. The same applies to newspapers, tires, plastic bottles, and metal cans. Nonetheless, state and federal governments have encouraged recycling by passing laws that require public agencies, newspapers, and other companies to purchase recycled materials. According to Tierney: "These regulations, along with a wide variety of tax breaks and subsidies, have pushed the national rate of recycling up to . . . [the] goal of 25 percent." But such regulations and economic incentives will never eliminate 100 percent of America's trash.

Tons of newspapers are readied for recycling.

Someday, new technologies may provide better ways to handle waste. Microwave systems are already replacing incinerators as the accepted way to eliminate certain types of medical waste. Perhaps scientists will eventually develop similar technologies to dispose of all forms of waste cleanly, safely, efficiently, and economically. Until then, people will continue to disagree over the most environmentally sound and cost-effective ways to handle America's garbage.

Chapter 4

Can Americans Afford Environmentalism?

GOVERNMENT ENVIRONMENTAL PROGRAMS LIKE those that support recycling, wilderness preservation, and endangered species protection cost taxpayers a great deal of money. But even more expensive are government environmental regulations.

Dixy Lee Ray and Lou Guzzo, in their book *Environmental Overkill: Whatever Happened to Common Sense?*, state that as of 1993, according to the Joint Economic Committee for the U.S. Congress, approximately 200,000 federal environmental regulations were in place at a cost of $115 billion annually to administer and police. The Environmental Protection Agency, which is responsible for enforcing many of these regulations at the federal level, estimates that current costs could reach $120 billion.

This amount does not include the cost of state environmental regulations, which are enforced by state environmental protection agencies. The largest such state agency in the nation, in California, has an annual budget of $255 million. The top ten state environmental protection agencies have a combined annual budget of a little more than $1 billion. These budgets, like those of federal agencies, are funded through taxpayer dollars.

Richard Morgenstern, in an April 1996 article published in *Environment*, explains how taxes affect the economy: "If a person earns $10 per hour and pays no taxes, he or she would have to work exactly one hour to purchase a new compact disc (CD) costing $10. With a marginal tax rate of one-third, however, the person would have to work an hour and a half to purchase the same CD."

Morgenstern adds that if the government enacts new environmental regulations that make the CD more expensive to manufacture, his hypothetical purchaser will pay even more for the CD:

> Now assume that an environmental policy is adopted to reduce toxic emissions from the manufacturer of CDs and that this raises the cost [to make the CD by] 2 percent, or 20 cents. . . . The person would have to work an additional 72 seconds (2 percent of 60 minutes) to purchase the CD.

Moreover, environmental regulations do not just increase the cost of manufacturing products. They also increase other business expenses. Ray and Guzzo explain that companies must fill out government paperwork, arrange government inspections, and do many other things to comply with environmental regulations, all of which "forces private firms to increase staffing, work longer hours, and add to mail, paperwork, travel, and phone expenses." Such expenses are often passed on to consumers.

The total cost of environmental regulations is high: Thomas Hopkins estimates that in 1995 alone, "American households, workers, and businesses spent $670 billion to comply with federal regulation." And Robert Stavins has concluded that Americans pay more for federal regulations than they do to support government environmental agencies:

> If we were to ask the general public what the economic costs of environmental protection are, people would respond in terms of what shows up in the budgets of government. . . . However, except for a rare number of public policies, those budget figures turn out to be a trivial part of the cost, anywhere from two to five percent or, sometimes, ten percent of the costs. More important are the [costs to businesses, which] constitute 80-90 percent of the true cost of environmental protection. These costs, of course, are passed on to consumers.

Ray and Guzzo believe that many politicians forget that it is difficult for the average American to afford these costs: "Perhaps it would help if more of the lawmakers and regulation writers had experience in trying to make a living in the private economy." They quote former senator, George McGovern who learned the true cost of government regulation only after going bankrupt. McGovern says:

> I wish that during the years I was in public office I had had this firsthand experience about the difficulties business people face every day. That knowledge would have made me a better U.S. Senator. . . . My business associates and I [have] lived with federal, state, and local rules that we all passed with the objective of helping employees, protecting the

environment, raising tax dollars for schools, protecting our customers from fire hazards, etc. etc. While I have never doubted the worthiness of these goals, the concept that most often eludes legislators is: Can we make consumers pay the higher prices for the increased operating costs that accompany public regulation and government reporting requirements with reams of red tape?

Some say no: They believe that consumers already pay too much for environmentalism. According to Ray and Guzzo:

Of course, everyone wants to avoid pollution and to improve on what has occurred in the past. But standards must be set that are reasonable and achievable. The policies and procedures must be practical without consuming so high a portion of disposable income.

Many critics of the environmental movement share the opinion that environmentalism is too costly. And many cite environmental laws and regulations as unnecessary. For example, in his book *No Turning Back: Dismantling the Fantasies of Environmental Thinking,* Wallace Kaufman says: "We have improved water and air quality and saved some important wild lands, but almost always with unnecessary expense and divisive political battles."

Similarly, Ronald Bailey, in his book *Eco-Scam: False Prophets of Ecological Apocalypse*, argues that unnecessary regulations are often the products of special interests that can obscure scientific truth. According to Bailey, scientists sometimes exaggerate environmental problems in order to get more money from the government so they can continue their work.

For example, he says, "in the 1980s, some climatologists began warning against an eroding ozone layer and catastrophic increases in the earth's average temperature. Subsequently, they have been rewarded with new grants of federal monies; the climate change research budget . . . climbed to $1.1 billion in 1992 and [increased] by 24 percent in 1993."

Bailey believes that these scientists probably exaggerated the problem for selfless reasons:

Most [scientists] believe in good faith that their work is important and possibly even vital for the future well-being of mankind. Therefore it is not surprising that some are tempted to try to attract more money by linking their efforts to whatever the latest crisis is. Thus the politicization of science has led inexorably to interest-group lobbying and to the erosion of the standards of objectivity, threatening the very foundations of the scientific enterprise.

The Ozone Layer

The issue of the ozone layer is frequently cited as an example of how "false science" has led to the enactment of unnecessary environmental laws and regulations. Ozone is a form of oxygen gas that occurs naturally in the upper atmosphere and provides a protective layer between the earth and the sun's radiation, and many scientists believe that this layer is thinning. They consider ozone thinning to be a serious problem because as the layer thins, the level of ultraviolet (UV) radiation reaching the earth's surface increases, and too much UV radiation can cause skin cancer in human beings.

However, Ray and Guzzo say that scientists are wrong to be worried about ozone thinning. They report that the density of the ozone layer normally fluctuates from day to day, sometimes as much as 50 percent. Therefore, "conclusions about long-term trends in the amount of stratospheric ozone cannot be based on single-day or short-term measurements."

Scientists do know that every autumn a "hole" normally forms in the ozone layer over the South Pole. Not actually a hole, the ozone in this region is 60 percent thinner than at other times; the phenomenon occurs over Antarctica because of a weather system called the polar vortex.

In the 1980s some scientists concluded that the hole was growing, and that the increased thinning was due to chlorofluorocarbons (CFCs), organic molecules in wide use at that time in industrial and commercial products such as refrigeration and air-conditioning units and some cleaning agents and spray propellants. Chlorine is a major component of CFCs, and Ray and Guzzo explain: "There is always a certain amount of chlorine present in the stratosphere, but it is believed by some atmospheric scientists that the stratospheric chloride that starts [the process of ozone destruction] comes from chlorofluorocarbons."

Consequently, the federal government banned the manufacture of CFCs, even though the ozone hole was first detected prior to the use of CFCs. In 1987 twenty-two other nations agreed to stop making or using CFCs. In May 1996 the National Oceanic and Atmospheric Administration reported a decline in CFCs throughout earth's atmosphere, and at an international forum on radiation that same year, researchers agreed that the ozone hole "has stabilized and should start to narrow in about a decade" because of the CFC ban.

But Ray and Guzzo say that it has never been proven that CFCs actually caused the ozone problem:

Although the presence of chloride appears to be directly involved in ozone breakdown, the origin of that chloride is open to question. The assumption that it comes from CFCs is based upon hypothesis only. . . . Chloride is one of nature's most abundant ions. Sea water evaporation provides the atmosphere with 600 million tons of chloride per year. Volcanic eruptions emit millions of tons of chloride. And at least another million tons of chloride are produced naturally every year.

Ray and Guzzo are not alone in believing that the CFC ban might have been unnecessary. For example, Stephen Hubbell, professor of ecology and evolutionary biology at Princeton University, is convinced that the ozone layer has not been appropriately studied, and he questions whether ozone thinning is really a serious problem. Even if the ozone is being depleted, he argues, how can scientists be sure it is a harmful process?

In a November 17, 1995, radio interview, Hubbell stated:

We've spent hundreds of millions of dollars to diagnose the existence of the ozone hole but we've spent only about 2% of that money to figure out if it makes any difference. That is, is the increased ultraviolet radiation that strikes the earth going to have any impact on the biosphere, on ocean fisheries,

The eruption of Mount St. Helen's released millions of tons of chloride into the atmosphere. Critics argue that the natural production of chloride is more detrimental to the earth's ozone than man-made CFCs.

forestry, agriculture, what? We don't know, and this is an example of no one . . . putting together a comprehensive study of the impact of ozone depletion on the stratosphere.

Some people believe that ozone thinning is responsible for a current increase in skin cancers. For example, Janice Longstreth of the Waste Policy Institute in Washington, D.C., says: "Fifty years from now, when ozone is back to normal, we could still have a wave of cancers because of the increase in [contact with radiation] we suffered earlier." But Ronald Bailey, in *Eco-Scam: The False Prophets of Ecological Apocalypse,* says that "the main risk factor [for skin cancer] appears to be severe sunburns in childhood rather than frequent exposure to UV."

Bailey quotes Dr. Alan Teramura, a botany professor at the University of Maryland: "There is no question that terrestrial life is adapted to UV. Even at a 20 percent decline in ozone we are not going to burn up all the plants on the surface of the earth or kill all of the people. We wouldn't see plants wilting or fruits dropping unripened on the vine."

Limited Environmental Dollars

Hubbell suggests that such disagreements indicate the ozone layer needs more study, and given America's limited environmental dollars, the country should not spend money on problems unless they are clearly identified:

> [I]n a fiscally conservative time when we have to cut our budgets [we need to] stand back and ask ourselves what do we really know about our environmental problems? And once we know that, we know what knowledge gaps we have to fill so we'll be much more intelligent about spending our research dollars in the future.

Likewise, Michael Fumento, in *Science Under Siege,* says that decisions on which environmental problems to spend money on must be based on logic rather than emotion:

> One cannot fear everything. Instead we make lists in our minds of those things we fear the most, fear less, and fear not at all. . . . The two major causes of premature death in this country are heart disease and cancer. Smoking, drinking, and overeating are the most efficient ways to die of one of those illnesses, along with getting sundry other maladies. These are public health enemies one, two, and three. Yet those of us who smoke, drink, and eat to excess find ourselves terrified of parts per quadrillion of headline-grabbing chemicals. . . .

> The chemical companies, big and faceless and run by [Chief Executive Officers] who sometimes make obscene amounts of money, make wonderful whipping boys, but it is amazing how many of us gladly ingest toxins and pollutants far, far worse for health than anything those companies have dreamed of pouring into the atmosphere or water. . . . Probably more people die from cigarette smoking in a day than have ever died from every chemical the Natural Resources Defense Council [environmental group] has rallied against.

Fumento says that people must think carefully before committing money to an environmental problem. When the government spends money on problems that might not exist, and businesses comply with environmental laws and regulations that might be unnecessary, he cautions, then environmentalism is not cost-effective and the entire U.S. economy suffers:

> It's true that American firms will be able to compete against other American firms no matter how onerous regulations become, simply because those other firms will have to comply with those same regulations. (Although small firms may be driven out of business because they will usually have less capital available to meet new requirements.) But if those regulation-strapped American firms must then compete with overseas businesses that suffer fewer controls, they will find that they cannot compete.

Fumento extends this reasoning to argue that if the economy suffers, then ultimately the environment will suffer, too:

> Because pollution controls are expensive, the best guarantee of being able to deal with pollution is to have an economy that is strong and a nation that's wealthy. It may be that in a country with no industry there is the least amount of pollution and environmental harm in the normal sense of the word, but the United States will never deindustrialize. . . . But among those nations that are industrial, it is the wealthy ones that have the least pollution.

In a 1996 editorial, economists Robert Krol and Shirley Svorny agree:

> Poor countries don't enforce environmental laws because they're trying to feed themselves. Researchers have found that, generally, income must rise above $5,000 per person before countries become wealthy enough to afford the luxury of constraining production in favor of clean air and clean water.

According to Robert Stavins, discussing environmentalism in terms of economics has polarized everyone involved with the issue. In his March 1996 *Quill* article, he states:

A plant in Tacoma, Washington, belches pollution into the air. Should the government stop such pollution, no matter what the cost?

Unfortunately, debates on environmental policy . . . have been dominated more by political positioning and ideological extremes than by reasoned consideration of the issues. The debate over potential use of benefit-cost analysis has been characterized by its proponents as "reforming a regulatory process that strangles the economy" and by its opponents as "ravaging essential environmental safeguards."

Stavins also points out: "Public demand for environmental quality may be greater today than ever before, but the costs of environmental protection have also reached unprecedented levels. Because of this, it is more important than ever that we try to achieve our environmental goals at the lowest possible cost." However, given such polarization, it is unlikely that people will ever agree on what those goals should be, on how much they should cost, and on who should pay for them.

Making Difficult Decisions

L AWMAKERS MUST MAKE DIFFICULT decisions regarding how to spend environmental dollars. There are many environmental problems to address, but when government agencies overspend on such problems, they increase the federal deficit. This jeopardizes the health of the American economy. As science and health writer Michael Fumento explains in *Science Under Siege:* "The United States economy is the largest and the most powerful in the world. It can take a heavy beating . . . but ultimately, struck hard enough, the economy . . . can be brought to its knees."

Fumento says that if environmental regulation continues at its current rate, ultimately it will be difficult for businesses to survive. He states: "The bottom line is that anything that diverts money away from business into something on which business would not spend that money is a drag on the economy."

Independent Science

Stephen Hubbell believes that the only way the United States can deal fairly with environmental problems is to create an independent, nonregulatory federal science institute called the National Institute for the Environment (NIE). The NIE would impartially identify and evaluate environmental problems, fund environmental research, and support the education and training of future environmentalists.

Funding for the NIE would come from the U.S. government, but the NIE would not operate its own laboratories. Instead, it would award research grants to top scientists in business and academic institutions, government laboratories, and nonprofit organizations. This independent approach will distance NIE scientists from the

politics of government agencies and environmental groups.

As the NIE proposal points out: "Whether justified or not, environmental research is often suspect when it is sponsored or conducted by regulatory or management agencies, which have agendas other than that of obtaining the best science. This is similarly true for research sponsored by industry and advocacy groups."

According to the Committee for the NIE (CNIE), the NIE would provide "a credible, independent source of scientific information" because it would be "insulated from the political influences typically experienced by federal agencies." Its scientists would concentrate on "identifying and setting long-range priorities and goals for [environmental] research and education."

Proponents of the NIE therefore believe that the institute would provide valuable objective information towards making environmental decisions. But these decisions would ultimately involve compromise by everyone affected by environmental issues: environmentalists, politicians, government agencies, businesses, and taxpayers.

Becoming Informed

But in order to decide when to compromise and when to remain committed to a position, people must become better informed about the costs and benefits of environmentalism. As John Gambro and

Harvey Switzky state in the April 1996 *Journal of Environmental Education:*

> Young adults, the next generation of voting citizens, will be required to make vital decisions on environmental issues. The general public is already taking an active role in policy decisions on environmental issues. Over the last several years, for instance, a series of popular referenda on nuclear power appeared on the general election ballots of various states. . . . If the citizenry is going to effectively confront such issues and make informed decisions, then they must be equipped with a fundamental knowledge of basic environmental concepts and processes.

In a January 1996 *Quill* magazine article, Robert Stavins says that the most difficult yet most important decision Americans must make regarding environmentalism is to determine "how clean is clean enough?" He offers this way of looking at the issue:

A crowd participates in a local Earth Day rally. Concern for the environment is at an unprecedented high, but the question remains as to whether such concern is valid.

Consider environmental policy decisions that we make in our homes when we decide about environmental control— for example, how often to sweep the floor in the kitchen. I don't keep my floor in an infinitely clean state. I don't invest all of my resources in keeping the floor clean. . . . On the other hand, I want to make sure that the floor of a surgical theater in which I might have an operation . . . [has] a much higher standard of cleanliness. The reason, of course, is that the marginal benefits of pollution control—preventing infection—are much greater in the surgical theater than in my own kitchen, where I tend not to carry out open heart surgery.

Americans must therefore consider individual environmental issues in terms of a broader agenda. Given that the U.S. government has limited economic resources, and that the public has only so much time and money to devote to environmentalism, people must decide which environmental problems deserve the most attention. In setting these priorities, they must balance competing environmental needs while still preserving the earth for future generations.

FOR FURTHER READING

Richard Amdur, *Wilderness Preservation*. New York: Chelsea House, 1993. Amdur discusses the destruction of wilderness areas throughout the world.

Edward F. Dolan, *The American Wilderness and Its Future: Conservation vs. Use*. New York: Franklin Watts, 1992. In discussing the American wilderness, Dolan talks about many land-use issues and laws.

Kathlyn Gay, *Garbage and Recycling*. Hillside, NJ: Enslow, 1991. Gay offers information about plastics, recycling, waste disposal, landfills, and NIMBY (not-in-my-backyard) groups.

Jake Goldberg, *Economics and the Environment*. New York: Chelsea House, 1993. An economist and environmentalist, Goldberg discusses the relationship between the two.

A. E. Sadler, ed., *The Environment*. San Diego: Greenhaven Press, 1996. This anthology offers a collection of articles on several important environmental issues.

Brenda Stalcup, ed., *Endangered Species*. San Diego: Greenhaven Press, 1996. This anthology offers a wide range of views on the pros and cons of the Endangered Species Act.

Jenny Tesar, *Endangered Habitats*. New York: Facts On File, 1992. Tesar offers many facts about endangered habitats and endangered species.

Terri Willis, *Land Use and Abuse*. Chicago: Childrens Press, 1992. Willis offers information about soil management and wise agricultural practices.

Works Consulted

Books

Ronald Bailey, *Eco-Scam: The False Prophets of Ecological Apocalypse*. New York: St. Martin's Press, 1993. A science writer and producer for the Public Broadcasting System (PBS), Bailey discusses several environmental myths and facts.

Alston Chase, *Playing God in Yellowstone: The Destruction of America's First National Park*. New York: Harcourt Brace Jovanovich, 1987. Chase talks about the deterioration of Yellowstone National Park and criticizes the role of the National Park Service in that deterioration.

Richard A. Denison and John Ruston, eds., *Recycling & Incineration: Evaluating the Choices*. Washington, DC: Island Press, 1990. Published by the Environmental Defense Fund, this book discusses waste management practices and policies.

Michael Fumento, *Science Under Siege*. New York: William Morrow, Quill Books, 1993. A critique of environmentalists and environmentalism's impact on American laws and taxes.

Robert Gottlieb, *Forcing the Spring: The Transformation of the American Environmental Movement*. Washington, DC: Island Press, 1993. An expert in urban planning, Gottlieb discusses the positive and negative aspects of both mainstream and grassroots environmentalism in America.

Wallace Kaufman, *No Turning Back: Dismantling the Fantasies of Environmental Thinking*. New York: BasicBooks, 1994. An award-winning scientist and critic of environmental groups,

Kaufman challenges many of the current philosophies of the environmental movement.

Jonathon Porritt, *Save the Earth.* Atlanta: Turner Publishing, 1991. This anthology discusses a variety of environmental issues from an environmentalist viewpoint.

Dixy Lee Ray with Lou Guzzo, *Environmental Overkill: Whatever Happened to Common Sense?* New York: HarperCollins, 1993. Ray, who has held many important political positions, including assistant secretary of the U.S. Bureau of the Oceans, joins reporter Lou Guzzo in criticizing many aspects of the environmental movement.

Susan Zakin, *Coyotes and Town Dogs: Earth First! and the Environmental Movement.* New York: Penguin Books, 1993. Zakin offers a history of the environmental group Earth First! and discusses the positives and negatives of the environmental movement as a whole.

Periodicals

Terry Anderson, "It's Time to Privatize," *World & I*, May 1, 1996. This professor of economics argues in support of the privatization of America's national parks.

Associated Press, "National Park Entrance Fees Will Increase to Fund Upgrades," *Los Angeles Daily News*, November 27, 1996. This article reports on entrance-fee increases in America's national parks.

Alan Attwood and Perry Bronwen, "New York Sniffs Out New Home for Its Rubbish," *Geodate*, vol. 9, July 1, 1996. Attwood and Bronwen discuss New York's shortage of landfill space.

Bruce Auster, Penny Loeb, et al., "The Color of Money," *U.S. News & World Report,* October 28, 1996. This article offers facts and figures regarding the money spent on the 1996 political elections, including expenses related to environmentalism.

Tom Bethell, "Species Logic," *American Spectator*, August 1, 1995. Bethell discusses the economics of the Endangered Species Act as it relates to the red-cockaded woodpecker.

Harry Blauvelt, "Only Congress Can Help," *USA Today,* September 19, 1996. Blauvelt supports more congressional funding for America's national parks.

Bill Bleyer, "$3 Boost in Fee to Visit TR's House: Extra Money Will Be Used for Maintenance," *Newsday*, March 13, 1997. This article reports on plans to raise fees to visit national historic sites, including President Theodore Roosevelt's Cove Neck home.

Christopher Boerner and Kenneth Chilton, "Making Recycling More Cost-Effective," *USA Today Magazine*, May 1, 1994. In their article about recycling, Boerner and Chilton quote Bill Brown, an executive at a waste management company.

Philip Brasher, "Forest Service Fees Too Low, Government Audit Says," *Los Angeles Times*, January 26, 1997, Bulldog edition. Brasher reports on a government audit that explains why forest fees are not high enough.

Eric Brazil, "A Changed Yosemite Now Open," *Los Angeles Daily News*, March 15, 1997. This article outlines changes in Yosemite National Park caused by flooding and a new management approach.

Bill Breen, "Getting Rid of Garbage. Burn It?" *Garbage,* vol. 3, March 1, 1991. This article talks about the pros and cons of trash incineration.

David Brittan, "Defending an Endangered Act," *Technology Review,* vol. 98, August 1, 1995. Brittan analyzes arguments in defense of the Endangered Species Act and the protection of the red-cockaded woodpecker.

Christopher Burns, "Crisis of Gigantic Size Looms as Europe Runs Out of Disposal Sites," *Los Angeles Times*, February 5, 1995. This article discusses trash management in Paris and other parts of Europe.

Alston Chase, "Secretive Expansion of Endangered Species Act Not Designed to Save Creatures," *Enterprise*, vol. 25, April 22, 1996. A critic of environmental groups, Chase argues against the proposed inclusion of hybrid animals on the endangered species list.

Frank Clifford, "Firms to Remove Lead from Faucets by 2000," *Los*

Angeles Times, September 1, 1995. Clifford reports on a lawsuit against faucet manufacturers requiring them to eliminate the use of lead.

Robert Devine, "The Little Things That Run the World," *Sierra*, July 1, 1996. Devine advocates the inclusion of more microorganisms on the endangered species list.

Mark Dowie, "The New Face of Environmentalism," *Utne Reader*, July/August 1992. From his position as an environmentalist, Dowie discusses the positives and negatives of mainstream environmental groups.

Maggie Farley, "Condor Conundrum: Plan to Reintroduce Endangered California Bird to Grand Canyon Area Angers Residents of Region," *Los Angeles Times*, April 28, 1996. Farley discusses the controversy over releasing California condors in Arizona and Nevada.

Stacy Finz, "Layoffs Hurt Immigrant Dream," *Los Angeles Daily News*, February 1, 1997. In reporting on the layoffs at a faucet-manufacturing company, Finz quotes several former workers.

John Gambro and Harvey Switzky, "A National Survey of High School Students' Environmental Knowledge," *Journal of Environmental Education,* vol. 27, April 1, 1996. This article discusses the need for people to become better educated about environmental issues.

James Gerstenzang, "U.S. to Promulgate New Guidelines Aimed at Protection of Wetlands," *Los Angeles Times*, November 30, 1996. Gerstenzang quotes environmentalists who say that new government wetlands policies are still not strict enough.

Tim Golden, "Yosemite Renewal Pondered," *Los Angeles Daily News*, February 2, 1997. Golden reports on Yosemite's 1997 flood damage and the controversy over how much of the park should be rebuilt.

Melanie Griffin, "They're Not for Sale," *World & I*, May 1, 1996. Griffin argues passionately against the privatization of America's national parks.

Garner B. Hanson, "Parks Belong to People," *USA Today*, March

10, 1997. This article argues that the government should not decrease tourist facilities at America's national parks.

Melissa Healy, "U.S. Parks: Not So Great Outdoors," *Los Angeles Times*, May 10, 1994. Healy reports on the crime problem in America's national parks.

Thomas Hopkins, "Cost-Benefit Paralysis," *National Review*, September 2, 1996. Hopkins discusses issues of cost and benefit as they relate to regulatory agencies like the Environmental Protection Agency.

Linda Kanamine, "Parks Are Seeking a Corporate Boost," *USA Today*, February 7, 1997. Kanamine reports on a National Park Service plan that encourages corporations to fund America's national parks.

Robert Krol and Shirley Svorny, "Price Pfister Woes Illustrate Hidden Cost of Pro-Environment Legislation," *Los Angeles Daily News*, December 8, 1996. From their perspective as economists, Krol and Svorny discuss the effects of environmentalism on businesses, particularly those in the faucet-manufacturing industry.

Thomas Lambert, "Endangered Species Act: Facing Stiff Opposition," *USA Today Magazine*, March 1, 1996. Offering several examples of the economic impact of endangered species recognition, Lambert talks about congressional opposition to the Endangered Species Act.

Stephen Lipske, "Finding a Future for an Endangered Bird," *National Wildlife*, vol. 34, April 1, 1996. An environmentalist, Lipske offers solutions to the problems of the red-cockaded woodpecker.

Kevin McNamee, "Pay Per View," *Nature Canada*, September 1, 1996. Writing in the magazine of the Canadian Nature Federation, McNamee explains how the Canadian government is trying to solve funding problems in its national park system.

Jeffrey A. McNeely, "The Expendable Future: U.S. Politics and the Protection of Biological Diversity," *Environment,* vol. 34, March 1, 1992. McNeely discusses the politics involved with promoting biological diversity, the Endangered Species Act, and the red-cockaded woodpecker.

Ken Miller, "Park Service Hammered Again over Management, Finances," *Gannett News Service*, March 7, 1995. This article talks about budget problems within the National Park Service.

Richard Morgenstern, "Environmental Taxes: Is There a Double Dividend?" *Environment*, vol. 38, April 1, 1996. An economist, Morgenstern analyzes the benefits of environmental taxation.

Paul Moses, "Winds Shifting on Fresh Kills," *Newsday*, November 30, 1996. Moses discusses the trash problem in New York City.

Robert Nelson, "The Future of the National Forests," *Society*, December 1, 1996. In this lengthy article, Nelson offers his opinions about how America should manage its national forests.

Robert Nelson, "Spotted Howls," *Reason*, vol. 28, June 1, 1996. A critic of environmental groups, Nelson discusses Alston Chase's book *In a Dark Wood: The Fight over Forests and the Rising Tyranny of Ecology*, and explains how the timber industry has been hurt by regulations to protect endangered species.

Sue Nelson, "Privatizing Looms as One of Many Dangers to Public Parklands," *Los Angeles Times*, May 7, 1995. Nelson argues against the privatization of America's national parks.

Newsday, "Yosemite's New Start: After Floods, a Yearning to Undo Human Imprint," March 10, 1997. This article reports on plans to limit tourist facilities in Yosemite National Park.

Mary F. Pols, "Not Condor Country," *Los Angeles Times,* April 28, 1996, Ventura County edition. Pols discusses opposition to the California Condor Recovery Program.

J. Winston Porter, "Long Island Topic: Should We Stop Recycling?" *Newsday,* September 8, 1996. Porter questions whether recycling is the best form of trash management for every community.

Mark Potok, "Free as a Bird in the Red-Rock Cliffs," *USA Today,* December 13, 1996. As a witness to an important condor release in Arizona, Potok reports on the successes of the California Condor Recovery Program.

Jerry Potter, "The Budget," *USA Today*, February 7, 1997. Potter offers an itemized list of federal budget allocations.

Nicholas Riccardi, "National Forest Visitors to Pay $5 for Parking," *Los Angeles Times*, February 19, 1997, Home edition. Riccardi reports on environmental-group opposition to a new national park fee.

Valerie Richardson, "Add Species to Endangered List," *Washington Times*, February 13, 1995. Focusing primarily on the red-cockaded woodpecker, Richardson reports on the impact of adding species to the endangered list.

Paul Rogers, "A Sight to See: Yosemite Attacking Backlog of Ills," *Los Angeles Daily News*, June 2, 1996. Rogers reports on the deterioration of Yosemite National Park as well as new projects to repair it.

Michele Salcedo, "Can Fresh Kills Close?" *Newsday*, November 4, 1996. Salcedo discusses the trash problem in New York City.

Neil Sampson, "It's Time to Reform ESA," *American Forests*, vol. 100, January 1, 1994. Sampson argues that the Endangered Species Act is ineffective in its present form.

Stephanie Simon, "Biologists Hope to Save Condors with 'Tough Love,'" *Los Angeles Times*, February 5, 1995. In reporting on an aversion program for California condors, Simon explains how condors benefit from human intervention.

Roger Starr, "Recycling: Myths and Realities," *Public Interest*, April 1, 1995. Starr analyzes the costs and benefits of various forms of trash management.

Roger Starr, "Waste Disposal: A Miracle of Immaculate Consumption?" *Public Interest*, September 1, 1991. Starr offers an in-depth discussion of trash incineration.

Robert Stavins, "Can Market Forces Be Put in Harness to Protect the Environment?" *Quill*, vol. 84, March 1, 1996. An economist, Stavins talks about the relationship between corporate profits and the environment.

Robert Stavins, "Economic Thinking in Environmental Coverage," *Quill*, January 1, 1996. In discussing the media's approach to reporting environmental stories as they relate to the economy, Stavins offers some excellent explanations of how the science of economics relates to environmentalism.

Barry Stavro, "Pacoima May Lose Fixture as Factory Shifts Jobs South," *Los Angeles Times,* October 1, 1996, Valley edition. Stavro reports on the closing of a faucet-manufacturing operation because of environmental regulations.

Barry Stavro, "Price Pfister Makes Cuts to Meet State Rules," *Los Angeles Times,* September 24, 1996, Valley edition. Stavro discusses the impact of environmental regulations on a faucet-manufacturing company.

Scott Steepleton, "A Better Balance for Wetlands," *Los Angeles Times,* December 9, 1996, Home edition. In discussing wetlands regulations, Steepleton briefly explains current wetlands definitions.

Richard Stroup, "Making Endangered Species Friends Instead of Enemies," *American Enterprise,* September 1, 1995. In discussing the red-cockaded woodpecker, Stroup explains how businesses can coexist with endangered species.

Shirley Svorny, "Landfill Capacity: A Problem We Can't Just Sweep Away," *Los Angeles Times,* May 19, 1996, Valley edition. Svorny reports on dwindling landfill space in Los Angeles, California.

John Tierney, "Recycling Is Garbage," *New York Times Magazine,* June 30, 1996. Tierney analyzes in depth several commonly held beliefs about recycling and questions whether the practice is cost-effective.

Tim Triplett, "Economics Meets Ecology as Recycled Paper Matures," *Marketing News,* vol. 28, February 28, 1994. Triplett explains the economics of recycling.

Jay Thomas Watson, untitled letter within Bob Baum's column, "A Rare Opportunity," *USA Today,* March 12, 1997. This regional director of the Wilderness Society argues in favor of eliminating some tourist facilities in Yosemite National Park.

Maura Weber, "Environmentalists File Appeal over New Wetlands Regulations," *Philadelphia Business Journal,* vol. 15, January 1, 1996. Weber reports on a major wetlands controversy in Pennsylvania.

Maureen West, "Yosemite Like Disneyland? No, It's a Wild, Wild World," *Los Angeles Daily News* editorial, July 23, 1996. In this editorial, West argues that wilderness areas can never be managed like amusement parks.

John Wood, "How Green Was My Balance Sheet," *Policy Review*, September 1, 1995. Wood analyzes the relationship between capitalism and environmentalism.

Speeches, Interviews, and Wire Service Reports

Adrian Croft, "Faucet Firms to Remove Lead in $2.8 Million Settlement, " Reuters News Service, January 30, 1996. Like Frank Clifford, Croft reports on a lawsuit to remove lead from household faucets.

National Public Radio's "Morning Edition" with host Alex Chadwick. "Interview with Dr. Stephen Hubbell," November 17, 1995. This discussion centers around environmentalism as it relates to economic issues and focuses on the establishment of a new environmental agency.

INDEX

Picture Credits

Cover photo: Jeffry Scott/Impact Visuals
AP/Wide World Photos, 33, 39
Archive Photos/Reuters/Joe Taver, 10
© Ira Berger/Woodfin Camp & Associates, Inc., 72
© Gary Braasch/Woodfin Camp & Associates, Inc., 40
© 1993 George Cohen/Impact Visuals, 55
Corbis-Bettmann, 60
© Robert Frerck/Woodfin Camp & Associates, Inc., 22
© Rick Gerharter/Impact Visuals, 58
© Lindsay Hebberd/Woodfin Camp & Associates, Inc., 38
© Sylvia Johnson/Woodfin Camp & Associates, Inc., 57
© 1990 Stephanie Maze/Woodfin Camp & Associates, Inc., 62
© Tom McKitterick/Impact Visuals, 51
National Park Service, 43; photo by Fred E. Mang Jr., 34
© Rick Reinhard/Impact Visuals, 75
© Alon Reininger/Woodfin Camp & Associates, Inc., 47
Southern Florida Water Management District/Gene Li, 31
UPI/Corbis-Bettmann, 69
U.S. Fish and Wildlife Service, 27; photo by J & K Hollingsworth, 19; photo by Ron Singer, 26

ABOUT THE AUTHOR

Patricia D. Netzley received a bachelor's degree in English from the University of California at Los Angeles (UCLA). After graduation she worked as an editor at the UCLA Medical Center, where she produced hundreds of medical articles, speeches, and pamphlets.

Netzley became a freelance writer in 1986. She is the author of several books for children and adults, including *The Assassination of President John F. Kennedy* (Macmillan/New Discovery Books, 1994), *Queen Victoria* (The Importance Of series, Lucent Books, 1996), *Alien Abductions* (Greenhaven Press, 1996), and *Butch Cassidy* (Mysterious Deaths series, Lucent Books, 1997). Her hobbies are weaving, knitting, and needlework. She and her husband, Raymond, live in southern California with their children, Matthew, Sarah, and Jacob.